SCOTTISH
FENCING

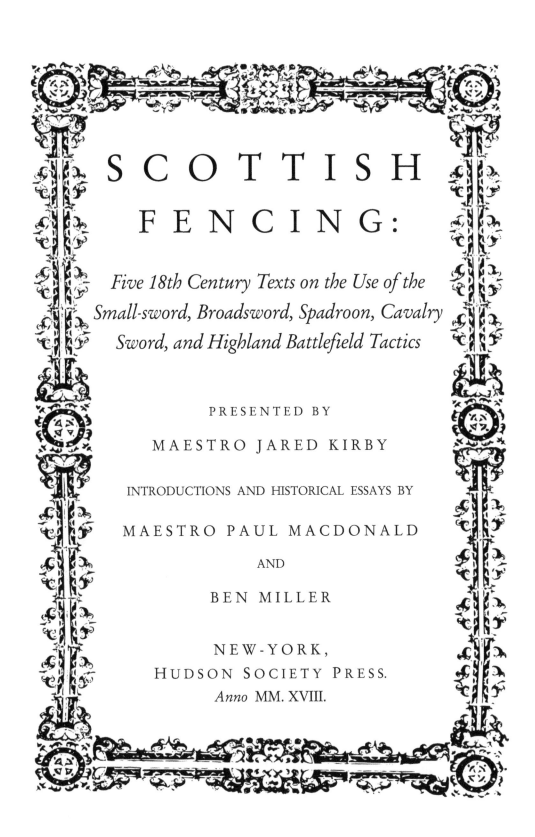

SCOTTISH FENCING:

*Five 18th Century Texts on the Use of the
Small-sword, Broadsword, Spadroon, Cavalry
Sword, and Highland Battlefield Tactics*

PRESENTED BY

MAESTRO JARED KIRBY

INTRODUCTIONS AND HISTORICAL ESSAYS BY

MAESTRO PAUL MACDONALD

AND

BEN MILLER

NEW-YORK,
HUDSON SOCIETY PRESS.
Anno MM. XVIII.

Front cover image of "Modern dress of a Highland Cheiftain, McNab Tartan + Clan Alpin Plaid, Black leather belt with dirk + pistol, Goat skin purse, ornamented with tasel, Broad sword" by George Walker, ca. 1792–1795, courtesy of the Yale Center for British Art, Paul Mellon Collection, Accession Number B1975.4.972.

Back cover image (hardcover edition only) of *The Guards of the Highland Broad Sword on the ancient Scottish principles* (Edinburgh: Oliver & Boyd, 1798) courtesy of the Anne S. K. Brown Military Collection, John Hay Library, Brown University.

Cover art and book design by Bronwyn Frazier-Miller.

Printed in the United States of America and the United Kingdom.

DISCLAIMER: The author, publisher, creators, and distributors of this book are not responsible, in any way whatsoever, for any loss, damage, injury, or any other adverse consequences that may result from the study, practice, or improper use made by any of the information or techniques contained in this book. All use of the information contained in this book must be made in accordance with what is permitted by law, and any damage liable to be caused as a result thereof will be the exclusive responsibility of the user. Many of the techniques described herein could lead to serious injury if not practiced under the guidance and training of a qualified instructor using appropriate safety equipment. This book is not a substitute for formal training. It is the sole responsibility of every person planning to train in the techniques described in this book to consult with a licensed physician before beginning.

Publisher's Cataloging-in-Publication data

Kirby, Jared. Miller, Ben. Macdonald, Paul.

Scottish Fencing: Five 18th Century Texts on the Use of the Small-sword, Broadsword, Spadroon, Cavalry Sword, and Highland Battlefield Tactics / Jared Kirby, Ben Miller, Paul Macdonald.

pages cm.

Paperback: ISBN 978-0-9990567-2-1

Hardcover: ISBN 978-0-9990567-3-8

1. Fencing. 2. Dueling. 3. Swordplay. 4. Martial arts—History—18th century. 5. Scotland—History. I. Kirby, Jared. Miller, Ben. Macdonald, Paul. II. Title.

FIRST EDITION

10 9 8 7 6 5 4 3 2 1

CONTENTS

ACKNOWLEDGMENTS

I want to thank Ben Miller for getting me involved in this project. Ever since the republication of Donald McBane's book (and Ben's introduction to that), I have found his level of research to be breakthrough in providing insight from primary source material that we haven't seen in hundreds of years. I know very few people digging this deep into the digitization of information on historical fencing.

For his transcription work, I would also like to thank Tony Mita.

As I read through this information in this book, I find such a rich reflection of Scottish culture and their martial arts. I think anyone interested in the martial arts of Europe will need to include this book in their library. I am glad to have helped in a small way and would like to thank Carol Kirby, Maestro Ramon Martinez and Maestro Jeannette Acosta-Martinez for their support over nearly the last two decades.

Jared Kirby
New York, September 2018

* * *

When, in October 2017, I first came across a reference to an anonymously authored Highland manuscript in the catalog of the Royal Library at Windsor Castle, I was intrigued as to what secrets it might yield, but was dubious as to whether the staff of a fabled institution such as the Royal Library would consider allowing a scan of its contents, or grant permission for me to publish a precious manuscript which had not seen the light of day in several centuries. Thankfully, my trepidation could not have been more in error, as the Royal Library kindly and graciously facilitated all of these wishes. In particular, for their immense assistance, I would like to extend my utmost thanks to Emma Stuart, Senior Curator of Books and Manuscripts, Oliver Urquhart Irvine, Librarian of the Royal Library, as well as the owner of the manuscript, the Royal Collection Trust and Her Majesty Queen Elizabeth II.

For their help in locating, scanning, and granting permission to publish the sketches of Donald McAlpine's backsword method (currently the earliest known illustration of fencing technique in America), I would very much like to thank the staff of the New Hampshire Historical Society—in particular, Wesley G. Balla, Director of Collections and Exhibitions, Malia Ebel, Reference Librarian/Archivist, and most especially, Sarah Galligan, Library Director.

Additionally, I would like to thank the following people:

Maestro Jared Kirby, for his invaluable support in the development of this book, and his assistance in obtaining many of the rare sources quoted herein.

Maestro Paul Macdonald, for lending his knowledge and expertise in discovering more information about the Royal Library manuscript's anonymous Highland author, and for contributing his outstanding and most illuminating introduction to this book.

Bronwyn Frazier-Miller, for her work on the book design and cover, as well as image restoration, and for her ever-steadfast love and support.

My fencing masters, Maestro Ramon Martinez and Maestro Jeannette-Acosta Martinez, for their continued mentoring in the art and science of fencing as well as in nearly all other things, and for their support, encouragement, and inspiration over the last thirteen years. Were it not for them, I would not be a fencer, nor would I ever have embarked down the path as a researcher and author of fencing-related texts.

Lastly, my parents, David and Pam Miller, as well as Jack and Pam Frazier, for their support throughout the years.

Ben Miller
Hollywood, September 2018

INTRODUCTION

Notes on *Examination & vindication of the Highlanders' manner of attacking and fighting the enemy in a day of action*

The Worlds of military history and historical fencing today should be indebted to Mr. Miller for bringing the following anonymous manuscript to published light.

Accounts second or third-hand and interpretations of historical works filtered through modern-day perspectives are all too common today. This discovery of first-hand battlefield accounts from three centuries ago is highly significant for several distinct reasons.

We firstly have the direct experiences of a war veteran laid before us. His style of writing alone tells us here that decades of professional military conflict have not stripped civility from this man in any way, but rather tempered his ability to learn from past actions and present his words with clarity and humility.

We secondly have vivid accounts of the Highlander and his arms in battle. Gaelic culture is rich with tales and legends of indigenous warriors and their indomitable spirit. This manuscript has been penned by a soldier who has heard their battle cries and known the sights and sounds of their very arms in action. Highland arms hold a somewhat unique fascination in our martial cultures, as the Highlanders stand yet as the last European warriors to use two-handed swords and sword-and-shield combination in battle.

Their holding fast to ancient ways comes from their inherent connections to traditions and the land. Their skill at arms, training from a young age and prowess in conflict formed the very Heart of Highland martial culture. For thousands of years, Highlanders have fought as warrior poets, and this spirit is captured and surmised succinctly by our anonymous soldier and author.

Thirdly, this work is one of great significance for the very fact that we hear the genuine feelings of a redcoat soldier expressing nothing but the deepest admiration for the Highlander, who has stood before him in past years as his own enemy.

This reason perhaps educates us on a deeper level than the mere technical or academic. When Jacobite conflict is portrayed, how often still today and with shallow thought, are pictures painted of "Barbarian Highlanders" facing the "English Redcoats"? With our more developed, collective knowledge today, we can now safely ascertain that neither terms are worthy of academic literature. This manuscript confirms exactly this, and was very much ahead of its time.

Our Brave author speaks of the disciplined nature of Highland Jacobite regiments, of the Art of their swordsmanship, of their officers bearing the "outmost Honour and integrity" and of their natural abilities as marksmen. These very attributes were only to be later borne out and publicly celebrated as Highland Regiments were formed within the British Army and fought resolutely in theatres of War worldwide.

What else can we learn from this?

From the author's descriptions, we can also ascertain certain details of his service Life and provide an estimation of the time of writing. His familiarity with military tactics and in particularly cavalry actions is clear. He speaks first-hand of experience at the Battle of Sherriffmuir in 1715 and again at the Battle of Dettingen in 1743. The Sherriffmuir action, where he speaks of the "..black Morass..." and specific cavalry movement around this, followed by personal knowledge gained from captured officers, confirms his part as serving with the Scots Greys.

The Scots Greys were a Scottish cavalry regiment who saw action at both Sherriffmuir and Dettingen. Their origins date back to 1678 and they played a role in suppressing Jacobite actions in 1689 (but did not play a direct battlefield role at the Battle of Killiecrankie, though this conflict is also mentioned by the author). From this information, we can now hear the words of a Scottish redcoat and one no doubt a Highlander himself in praise of those also from his own native land and culture.

In terms of dating the manuscript, the latest date attributable from the text would be that of the Battle of Dettingen (27 June 1743). Given also that the primary subject of the manuscript is praising the Highlanders in battle, there is, however, one reference that is conspicuous by its absence—Culloden.

It could be suggested that the last battle of the Jacobite Risings may already have occurred, and this might be a deeper compulsion for the author to remorsefully praise his fellow Highlanders. This notion is romantically compelling until we consider the author's reference, "And as for use of Arms tis true they have been forbidden the publick use of them for some time." He further confirms, "...the last time they were in arms in the year 1715..."

The Disarming Act came into force in the Highlands of Scotland from November 1716 onwards, following the 1715 Rising. The mention of "some time" passing since disarming combined with a lack of reference to Culloden (and of the '45 Rising in any form) gives us a more realistic period of writing between July 1743 and August 1745.

In this sense however, and at that time, the Heartfelt emotional support from a Government soldier to Highland men-at-arms carries an unknowing aura of the darkest irony for what was yet to come.

From first-hand battlefield experiences seen through the eyes of a young cavalry soldier, to penning his deepest sentiments in praise of his native warriors, now here it is published the first time for your own eyes.

We should be grateful for soldiers with stories, cultural pride, written records, material preservation and our technological age today which might breathe Life once again into all of these.

Paul Macdonald,
Highlander and Army Reservist
Master-at-Arms, Macdonald Academy of Arms

The following fragmentary manuscript is presented here with the permission of the Royal Library at Windsor Castle, where it resides under the following inventory number and title:

RCIN 1083485, *Examination & vindication of the Highlanders' manner of attacking and fighting the enemy in a day of action.*

The contributors wish to extend their utmost thanks to the staff of the Royal Library at Windsor Castle for making the publication of this transcription possible.

Examination & Vindication
of the Highlander's Manner
of attacking and fighting the
Ennemy, in a Day of Action.
by...
XI:38:36.

an <u>Examination</u> & <u>Vindication</u> of the Highlander's <u>Manner</u> of attacking and fighting the Ennemy, in a Day of Action,

The knowledge I have of the Highlanders and the just value I have for them is such that I cannot without some pain hear people speak of them with contempt especially about their fighting and look upon them as far inferior to the regular forces; I know that the Error prevails very much both in England and Scotland, as also in other places. But as that only happens in those places where their value is not known, I have often wished that somebody would set their practice in such a light as might stop people's discourse by letting them know how good soldiers they are. But as I do not see any body was like to under take such a task I thought it incumbent upon me to do it. And tho' tis not a thing I think I can do as well as I could wish, or the subject deserves, yet I thought it was better do it, as well as I Can than leave it undone, I have one advantage in it, that the thing is so

Clear in itself that there is nothing to do but to represent matter of fact. And the people in reading these sheets may say that it was done by a bad hand, yet I am persuaded that the little I say will convince them that the thing is convincing in itself and would have been much more if it had been presented by a better pen.

The opinion that people commonly have of them is that they are stout clever fellows tis true, and that even no body can deny them both Good heart and good will but that at best they are but Militia and what can a parcel of men without Discipline or regularity do against regular forces and disciplined troops which opinion I shall examine.

And show both by Theory and experience I hope to the conviction of a Man, that not only the Highlanders are as good as any regular Troops but that there is no Troops in Europe but they have the advantage of in the Day of Battle. And that tho' they cannot dance throug their Exercise like the English red Coats yet they have discipline enough to keep their Ranks, and obey their superior's Commands. And that in regard of the rest, the very irregularity with which they make their attack upon the Enemy, is the thing that gives it the more impetuosity, and makes it the more irresistible; And that if two sets of Men were equal in everything else, and the one arm'd and fight in the Highlander way, and the other fight in the way now made use of by the regular Troops; tis absolutely imposible but the Highlanders must prevail, which will seem to be a very odd thing to those that are so fond of regular Troops : But will appear absolutely clear to a Mathematical Demonstration when they examine the thing to the bottom as I have done.

In the first place, I shall show what advantage their way of attacking, gives them to break the Ranks of the Enemy; And I shall next show what advantage, the kind of Arms they carry, gives them, when by having penetrate into the Enemy's ranks they come to a class Engagement or what the french call, <u>la mélée</u>, I shall thereby answer to some objections, made against them, and show that those faults, are not so much essential to, and inseperable from the Highlanders in general; as only occasioned some Circumstance or other, which might easily have been remedied before, and might easily be prevented for the future, if ever they were brought into the Feild again to serve their King and Country.

But before I speak any thing about them, it will be necessary to make such a Description of their arms, and their way of fighting, as may be understood; which I hope to do to the conviction of any Body, that has had occasion to be in the feild with them.

A Highlander carries to the feild a gun, a broad sword and a Targe, a pistol on his belt of one side, and a Dirk, which is a Medium betwixt a poynard and a hanger of the other side.

As for the gun it is what the Highlander depends least upon; all the use of it, is to terrifie the Enemy; who if they thought that there was no fire against them, might keep up their fire, till the Highlanders were just at the end of their Muskets, and demolish them altogether; And yet at the same time every body will own that has seen the Higlanders in an Engagement that they do by far more execution, even with it, than the regular Troops; But all that they either expect, or can wish, is to bring it to an equality by giving fire of both sides at once, as near as posible which they can only do, by keeping up till the Enemy has fired, and firing immediately after them, as soon as they have done they throw by their guns and leave them in the feild, and draws their broad swords, and then begins the confusion; for immediatly every man takes a Race and runs as fast as he can in upon the Enemy; but as every body must own, that it is Imposible for Men to keep their Ranks when they go above a certain Pace, because every body cannot go equally fast, And them that go Slow, cannot come up as soon as them that go fast.

So after that, they do not mind their Ranks, but every Man attacks the Enemy, as he happens to come up with them; but as they cannot all get Room in the front, Them that come fast and find themselves in the Rere, by pushing foreward to get at the Enemy, push them that are before them; which adds a great deal of weight to the impetuosity with which they came upon the Enemy, and helps them much to push down the Enemy's ranks and break in upon them: But as they (as I said before), do not come regularly nor equally in, so they do not make the Line against the Enemy equally thick, but in some places there will be a dozen or twenty men, all in a heap, maybe 5 or 6 men thick, all pushing one another forward, and in other places for a good space the line will be very thin; And as tis very natural to think, that as the Enemy's line is equally thick in all it's parts (that is to say) three men thick, which it is commonly, those parts of the Highland Line, that are five or six thick, will sooner bear down that part of the Enemy's line that they engage than that that is but one or two thick. But then those that have penetrate through, turn to the Right and Left and flank those of the Enemy, that are still keeping their ground, against them that are attacking them of front; and every body will own them that they have but a bad chance when they are attacked so on all sides and that they must all be destroyed or put to flight.

But it will be objected to me here, that I am begging the question, and that I am supposing, that they will bear down the Enemy's line which is the question in dispute; Against that objection, I shall bring no worse proof than a Mathematicall demonstration; for any body that understands anything of Mechanicks, will know that in case that of two equall bodys, the one be standing still and the other be moving hard against it, tis a certain demonstration that the Body that is moving will beat away the body that is standing still, and push it out of its place and that the faster and the quicker it comes upon that Body, the easier it will push it away, which is exactly the case betwixt the Highlanders and the regular forces, Since the quickness with which they run in upon them, gives the impulse they make against them, that velocity which every body that knows the Laws of Motion, must own will add a great deal of force to the impetuosity of their attack; But if the body which moves with velocity should happen to be by far heavier than the body against which tis pushed, by the same rules of Mathematicks, it must have a far greater force than ever it had before, in proportion to the odds of weight, that it has more than the body in opposition to it, which is quite the case with the High-landers.

For as I said before that, that part of the line that was thinnest might be withstood, e contrario, it must be allowed, that that part which is thicker and by consequence heavier, must be irresistible: there is something more to be said in regard of the impetuosity of their attack, but as it cannot be understood before I have said something of their arms I shall leave it for another Article.

As a demonstration such as I have been bringing cannot be contradicted nor controverted, the only shift those that argue against the Highlanders will have, will be to evade it by saying that such an Argument may hold good betwixt two inanimate Bodies, or which is the same case to Bodies deformed, whereof certainly the greatest crowd, must bear away the least; but that is quite a different thing, when Men are armed, And that the the regular forces with their bayonets at the end of their Guns would soon stop their carreer, or put an end to their impetuosity with their Lives; But this is quite a wrong notion, for as they have targes to receive the stroak of the Bayonets upon, it can do them no more harm, than if they did not get it at all; So that the Bayonets by that time are of no more use to the regular forces than if they were unarmed.

Which brings it to the case in which nobody can deny, but the Mathematicall Demonstration holds good, And which as I think I have made clear to a Demonstration, gives the advantage to the Highlanders tho they had no other to depend upon; But that is not all, for tho' the Enemy's Arms are made useless by their defensive arms, they have offensive arms that the Enemy has no defense against, I mean their Broad Swords, with which at the same time, they receive the Stroak of the Bayonetts upon their targes, they bestow such stroaks upon the Enemy as soon put them out of condition of resisting; for in the new way of fighting as the regular forces depend merely upon their offensive arms, they provide no defensive arms, So that if once you make their offensive arms useless they have nothing more to depend upon; which gives the Highlanders the greatest advantage that can be when by the help of the targes they have got so far within reach, of the point of their bayonetts as to make them useless as I said before.

And I assure you that they make very good use of the advantage they have; for they have such a particular Art in handling a Broad Sword, that a stroak given by them will do much more execution then a stroak given with the same force by any body else, so that it happens that there is very few of the regular forces that are attacked by them but must receive deadly Stroaks from them being defenseless, whereas there is as few of the Highlanders can be hurt by the regular forces, which makes it that I can compare them to nothing else by an unarmed man, or a sett of men, fighting against a full armed Enemy, for tis the same thing to be unarmed as to have such arms as the Enemy can render useless.

I think now the paradox begins to appear in a clearer light and any body may conceive how tis possible for a tumultuous attack to get the better of a regular line, both by breaking their Ranks with ease, and doing execution after they have penetrated into them; But there is one thing more which any body that knows anything of warr must absolutely own; Which is that as tis the greatest disadvantage imaginable for troops to part with their fire too soon so tis the greatest advantage in the world for one party to keep up their fire like they be close at the Enemy which last is the case with the Highlanders, for as I said in the Description of their Arms, every one of them if they be full armed has a pistole by his side and tho he be willing to give fire with his gun as soon as his Neighbours, yet it is a fundamentall principle amongst them which they never have any notion of going against as

{Note: In the original manuscript the pages numbered "9" through "16" are missing}

As much as all the 3000 had done; for the 3000 without Cannon could do no more, and he kept these two or three thousand Men at this fine exploit, at the time that he might have been over running the whole country with them; For at the time he gave these orders there was not 500 men in all Scotland to oppose him; 'till by keeping his men useless he allowed them to come down by parcells from England, and gather tho' very slowly, to the number that came to the Sherriff moor.

In which tis commonly supposed, that the Highlanders were defeat, but falsely since it was quite otherways, as will appear to any Body that knowes the circumstances of that Engagement and will render upon them impartially.

In the first place I shall own, that the Highland left wing was beat by the right wing of the regular Army, but every body knows that their Right wing again got the Victory over the Left wing of England, and routed them so far, that there never was one of them rallied again, so that they changed places in the field of Battle, and the Highlanders at least the Right wing of them that were at the south side of the Moor in the Morning found themselves at the north side after the Engagement and the Duke of Argile who commanded the English and by having pursued the wing he had routed was get on the south side from from the North side where he was before, was so far from choosing to attack once more the part of the Highland Army, that was still standing, that he took the shortest call to retire to Stirling a strong town in the Neighbourhood, and left them, not only upon the feild of Battle, but upon the very ground he had drawn up upon in the Morning, whereas the Highlanders thought them selves so strong, that when the saw him marching off, it was proposed in a Council of War held in the feild for that purpose to attack him upon his retreat; but tho' the generality were for it, yet twas carried to the contrary, by some of the prevailing people, under pretext that the men were fatigued and that they would have a better occasion another day; in which they were far mistaken for the English, kept themselves within their camp under the Common of Sterling til by disappointments and misconduct the Highland Army dwindled so far that they could never make Head again, but in the mean time I do not believe that anybody will say that that Army is beat, that keeps the Feild of Battle and that those are the conquerors, that choose to retire; And I believe most people are persuaded and I do not doubt that most of the English Army, that were there will own that if they had seen the Highlanders coming down upon them from the top of the Moor, they would have retired faster than a step; at least the prisoners that were taken declare that they had heard them speak as if they were upon that Resolution, and if I own it to be a drawn Battle, I think it is all that can be expected; And in the next place I shall show that that part of the Battle, that was lost, was not lost by the Highland men, for in that Wing that was beat, there was no more but one single Batlalion of the true Highlanders, or what is called the clans the rest being all composed of the low country men, that are not by far so good troops as them and at most Batalions of those people that have upon the edge of the Highlands, and are at mixture between the two, in so that they never were intended to be in the first Line, but were intended to be in the second Line, as the worst troops of the Army, and were sent up to the fist Line in the marching up to the Enemy, by a confused and misplaced command of the General who was at the head of that part of the Army, and which was so sensible an Error in him, that the very Gentleman who was to carry the order, and who was an officer that had seen a great deal of service in the regular way, represented to him, that it was too late for him to give such an command and that is was impossible for troops that knew nothing of Evolutions to change the order they were in, in such a suddenly as he expected, and that he was afraid it would put them in confusion, but that if he would allow them to go on in the order they were in, he believed it would answer better; his answer was that when he was a General he should get leave to command, but in the meantime he desired him to obey, which was so positive an answer, that he could not say anything more against it, but it happened just as he had fore seen, for that Body of troops which was drawn up in a very regular way to be the second Line, and had nothing ado, but to march up in the order they were in, being commanded to divide in columns, for to march up to the Enemy, and form again into a Line for the attack, instead of doing it in a regular way as he intended, did it so confusedly that the host that were upon them left to support them, were thrown into the center, and they were thrown not only upon the Wing so far out of the place they should have been in, that instead of covering the first line as was intended, they were in a manner a separate Body by themselves, so that the very Horse of the Enemy's right wing that was drawn up against the first Line was obliged to march to the right and draw up with great divisions betwixt every squadron, for fear of being out winged by the Host that they saw coming against them; which motion out the regular Horse so much out of order that that same might have been an advantage; for it was the opinion of the most part of the Gentlemen that had the misfortune to be there, that even in the Confusion they were in, if they had been commanded to advance briskly upon the Enemy's horse whilst they were in the disorder the new motion to a side had just put them into, they would easily have put them to flight, but the General, whose name was Hamiltoun, who had given the wise command, that had already put them in confusion instead of staying to try to repair his mistake, and to make the best he could of the men in the order they were in, which he probably might have done to a very good purpose, considering the disorder the unexpected motion, the Enemy's horse had been obliged to make had put them into but instead of that he choosed to take panick and run away before even the Battle began, and the poor men were obliged to stand still forward of Order to attack not only till the Enemy were formed a new, but for want of being hurried on as new soldiers should be, the panick grew upon them to such a degree, that at last they could stand it no longer, but after a great many poping shots they gave a full fire, and immediately ran away.

There was too another advantage which might have made up for all the mistakes that had happened, if the General had but stayed to make use of it which was that there happened to be betwixt them and the Enemys horse a kind of black Morass, which is very common in our Moors, which hindred the horse to come at them, to break them, because if they had attempted it they would have sunk into the Morass, whereas if the foot (who could have easily gone through it, because twould have supported the foot though it could not support the horse) had but advanced as far as they would have done without fear of the horse they would soon have made them retire, with their shot; for every body knows, that the only advantage of the horse consists, in a sudden attack, and that if by any accident or the situation of the ground (as in the case here mentioned) they are hindred from it, tis impossible for them to stand long the fire of the Infantry, so that very accident might have won the Battle. And to show the verity of what I say concerning the situation of the ground on that occasion, every body knows that even when the Infantry of the Highland army ran away, the horse were obliged to go a good way round, before they could find ground firm enough to get over to pursue, which gave the most part of the men an opportunity of escaping so that almost none were taken prisoners, but the Gentlemen that were there as officers, who not choosing to run away with their men stood till they were taken prisoners, and it was from some of them people that are known to be of the outmost Honour and integrity that I got the averment I have given concerning it.

Now I shall be leave to say that it was not the Highlanders that were beat but the Low Country men; but tho they had been the best men in the World, would it have been surprising? considering how they were mismanaged, not only to get wrong orders before the Battle but also to be without any General at all during the time of it, that would so much as give them orders to charge at a proper time or by some other contrivance repair the fouls he had committed at the beginning which one may see by what I have said just now he might easily have found an opportunity of doing; And I shall ask if any Army in the World can either fight, or be unanimous in any one Resolution whatsoever, if they have not somebody to give orders to the whole? For every one says that they should march foreward whilst the Enemy was in disorder, but no body could take upon them to do it without orders from the General, who by that time was on his way home again, and had left the men in the lurch; and therefore I think this cannot much contradict what I said, since it should only be imputed in part to the Low Country men, (whom I do not pretend to be so good as the Highlanders far from it); but much more to their General whereas the other wing as it happen'd to be, tho it was intended for the whole of the front line, having the good luck to have at their head an experienced oficer, who had been long in foreign service and who had both the courage and Resolution to attack afoot, at their Head (which gives commonly the Highlanders great Sports) And besides the prudence to require nothing of them but what he knew they could execute, which was to march boldly up in the order they had been drawen in at first, and to attack briskly after they had given their fire; They I say routed so thoroughly the part of Argile's army that was before them, that there never was one of it that rallied or appeared in the feild again, but were almost all cut to pieces, with the terriblest slaughter that could be imagined, and the very few that escaped, ran to Sterling, their headquarters, and carried news that the day was lost; what happened after the Battle such as the Duke of Argile's not daring to attack a second time, but leaving them on the feild of Battle and returning under the cannon of the castle of Sterling; And their missing the opportunity of defeating him upon the Retreat under frivolous pretences, I have spoke of before, so that I need not repeat it; But that shows that even in this Battle we did not safe the Victory, and that it was at most a drawen Battle, and that if there had been no Engagement, but in that Wing where the Highlanders engaged, the advantage would have been undoubted of their side upon that occasion as well as all others, And if what I have said can but prove that the Highlanders are thorough Good Men and entirely to be depended upon; I shall willingly own that the the Low Country men are not so which is all that can be concluded from the loss was sustained upon that occasion; there are a great many other occasions in which the Highlanders have showen their courage and the advantage they had over the regular forces some of them even since the Battle of Sherriffmoor which would be too long to report here, especially since I think I have said enough to show that experience at least is of their side, and that whatever might have happened to the Low Country men, the real Highlanders at least were never defeat, and that these troops, that always got the Victory as yet should have a chance to do so again, therefore I shall say nothing more upon that subject.

But the next thing that remains to do is to answer some objections that I have heard made against them which I shall do in as short terms as I can.

In the first place it will be said that whatever the Highlanders might have been heretofore, they have been now so long out of the use of Arms that they cannot be anything like to what they were, that seems to be a very plausible objection, but before I undertake to answer it, I shall examine the meaning of that expression viz' to be and of the use of Arms and then I shall examine, whether other people that think they have a great advantage over them, upon that score are not as much and even more out of the use of Arms than they are in the proper sense of the word.

In the first place whether is it the proper sense of being in use of arms to dance through one's exersize with a Musket in one's hand and to fire so many pluffs, with blunt shot at a word of command upon the esplanade of a Garrison to war, or in Hide park? or whether is the real sense of the word to have seen fire in earnest in the face of an Enemy, and by often having been in the occasion of danger, to learn not to be more afraid of it than is necessary, and even then only thereby to be the more encouraged to act with coolness and presence of mind to oppose it and turn it upon one's Enemies? And after they by experience have acquired such a sedatory, and as I said before, presence of mind, whether the real use of arms be not to keep up one's fire til till the Enemy be within such distance as it will have effect, instead of giving it whilst they are yet at such a distance that not one shot out of 100 will either hit or do execution? of these I believe every body that knows anything of war will own, be the real sense of the word I would wish to know of what use parading and plattooning at a Review, was to the armys of the two Nations in Europe that are looked upon as having the most natural courage at the Battle of Dettingen. And whether they did not fire and act upon that occasion as rashly as if they had never either seen or heard tell of firing a Gun? But before I say anymore about it I shall say something of the Highlanders In regard of their natural courage and the use of arms, that their way of Living brings them into. In the first place no Nation in the World has less notion of the fear of an Enemy in general, or of regular forces in particular, and the reason of it is that them that are come to any age have tried them, both at Killycrankee and at Sherriffmoor, and for the younger ones, they are so much encouraged by the story, that the old people tell them both of the late Engagements they have seen, and of these they have heard described by their Fathers, and from tradition, that they think no more of encountring regular forces than if they were to go through a herd of sheep; And if they were so hurried on an attack so as not to get time to think otherways, I am persuaded that it would answer now as well as ever it did; for as for the fire of the regular forces they have heard so often how little execution it did that they think no more of it before hand than if it was pop guns, and that very notion Will make them stand it, if that was once over is realy reason for them not to fear anything else as I have said before; And as for use of Arms tis true they have been forbidden the publick use of them for some time, and that they neither are so common amongst them not were those that had them allowed to wear them in publick, such as, at markets and other publick meetings yet tis known to every body that there was few of them but made use of them in private such as shooting at game, which is very common upon their Hills, and that there is almost none of them but has been at that trade very often, and very few of them but are exceedingly good marksmen, and the guns be much rarer amongst them, than they were yet they contrive always some way or other to practize them; I suppose that them that have lend them to the rest in so far that I have heard even even the officers of the regular army say that those amongst their soldiers that were Highlanders (for some there are that are for Bread obliged to engage amongst them) were all exceeding good marksmen from their very first arrival at the Regiment, when the Low Country men even those that had been long in the Regiment were quite the contrary, which makes me hope that even in the first fire itself not withstanding what is thought of the Regular forces the advantage would be of the Highland side, and after that was over, I am very sure it would be out of question, for as to the Broad Sword and Targe the use of them is so natural to them, and so easie especially against a Bayonett that there would be no difficulty in it, not no fear of their using them to very good purpose. But as I said I would speak again of the Battle Dettingen, I shall bring the thing as far into a practice in regard to the Highlanders as a thing can be allowed to be carried on by suppositions; And as the English upon that occasion were said to have a kind of advantage, I shall only speak of it in regard of them that had the better; every body knows that the whole line gave their fire before the Enemy was within three times the distance commonly allowed for a Right fire in a Battle, and that if the Enemy had advanced quick enough upon them they would have all been broke as they were in that part where the Musquetairs attacked them, and whether would the Highlanders have desired a better game to play than the attacking them in those circumstances.

I remember some time after that Battle I heard an English Officer bragging of the Victory they had obtained and speaking of the coolness of the English soldiers upon that occasion say he heard one of them say to his Neighbour by God Jack we have given the last fire a great deal too soon but we must take better care to give this to better purpose and in a more proper time; I do not remember whether I thought proper to answer him, but I remember very well that what occurred to me then was that if the English or and other Troops were in opposition to the Highlanders, and were so kind as to bestow the first fire upon us early enough we would not quite give them long time to consider what they were to do with the second.

But I cannot omitt speaking here something concerning the attack of Horse against foot, every body knows that if foot part with their fire and allow the horse to attack them upon equall terms, that is to say without fire of either side the horse have an absolute advantage over them not withstanding their Bayonetts as was seen, at that affair in that place where the Musqetairs attacked and what is it that gives them the advantage, nothing but the impetuosity of their attack that is to say the velocity in which they run and the superior weight with which they fall upon them, which is in so far the case of the Highlanders; For as the Horse only come in at a large trot, the Run that the Highlanders take is every bit as quick if not quicker then it and tho they have not so much weight as the horse, which makes that they cannot peirce them so quick as they do yet their going in waves or platoons gives them weight far superior to the Resistance of the Enemy's line, and besides they help themselves foreward by cutting their way through with their Broad Swords so that tho they do not break them so suddenly yet they do it as effectively and to much better purpose for the horse by the force with which they come ride them down its true but then they cannot stop amongst them to make use of their advantage by killing them because the same impetuosity that brought them in carries them foreward so that they have them almost untouched to rally again unless they be supported by foot coming after them, which may not allways answer, whereas the Highlanders as they have not quite so much impetuosity when they break in upon a line, they stick better to it and instead of running through it, they turn to the right and left according as they break in and destroy all that stands against them till they meet their Neighbours that are doing the same thing towards them, and what escapes the first attack, which is commonly very few (for once they get in their execution is so quick that they give time to very few to run away) these they either drive upon the second line or pursue so hard as to overtake them and kill them in the distance that's betwixt the two Lines, so that in case they should not break the second line which they often will do by attacking them in the surprise that the defeat of the first line puts them in they will at least have full room to relive and rally again, which some people say they cannot do, but I do not know upon what foundation for I do not remember any occasion, in which they have failed to do so, but that unluckie one of the left wing at the Sherriffmoor, but I doubt whether even the Regular forces would have rallied when they were totally defeat as they were and pursued by Cavilery without having the advantage of a second line to stop the pursuers, so that that can be an example. But to return I cannot omitt remarking that in attack they have the advantage of both horse and foot for they are as good as horse by their impetuosity in attacking and as good as for doing execution after the line is broke, And as good again as horse for pursueing the runaways, and whether that be not advantageous Troops, that are as good as horse and foot, both joined in one, I refer to any body; they have one advantage more which horse have not, which is that for as terrible as horse are to foot, after the fire is over, yet if the foot will keep up their fire, horse can do nothing to them, but must retire before them, whereas the Highlanders not only are equall, to the foot, but even have the advantage of them, if both by like experience of a Campagne or like were brought to so much coolness as to make best use of their fire, And I am persuaded that they will be as soon brought to it as any other troops that I know which is that tho Highlanders should by accident part, with their fire once, the foot tho' they intended to attack them with the advantage of Charged Guns advance so slow when they attack that we would probably have time to charge again before they came at us, and by consequence receive them still upon equall terms, whereas if ever they part with their's they are gone because we on the contrary always advance so quick upon them that they never can get leave to charge again, and if once we come within swords length of them there is no fear of them troubling us again for awhile, for the Highlanders demolish so far those troops that the once get the handling of, that they seldom appear in the feild again for a good while, it is true that people will say that they will fire in platoons so as still to be giving us some fire and yet have always fire to receive us with they are very welcome even to do that for, as for the slowness of their advancing, we can venture to give full fire whilst they are only, give platoons, and as common way of firing in platoons is on platoon of three or at most two over the whole line it makes up but one third or at most a half of their fire and if we give them a full fire every time we receive the third or half of theirs it will come in my calculation to our giving them at least two if not three full fires for one, and I doubt whither they will not fire first at that rate so that the Highlanders have the advantage of foot even in that shape as well as all the rest.

I know there will be several objections made in regard of what I say here, but their attacking us so much slower than we do them gives us so much the advantage of time for our recharging that I doubt whither there will be many occasions where my proposition will not stand to the full, and I am sure there is none, where it will not stand good, at least in a great measure, and if any objection be made to it I am ready to bring it to such a calculation in proportion of time as I am pretty sure will convince any man, tis true they behoved to be very good soldiers and very much Masters of their Temper to take the time so exactly as to execute these to advantage, but I said before that it would be only necessary when both partys were growen so by experience and in the mean time till their Enemy was grown very good troops indeed they have so many advantages other ways that they needed not be at the trouble of trying this, so that they needed not try it 'till they were capable to execute it.

There is one thing that we can do that is impossible for the regular troops, and against which I am sure there can be no objection and tho it has never yet been tryed, yet I am persuaded that both the feasiblness of the project and even the usefullness will appear plain to any body; every body knowes that the only use of the second line is to support the first, that is to say when tis broke to allow the soldiers to retire through the intervals of the second line to rally, and then the second line becomes the first and either receives the attack of the Enemy that were pursueing the first line or advances to attack them as they are desired, that at least is what is expected from them, but does the effect allways answer as one could wish and does it not very often happen that when the first line is just to flight the runaways instead of having time to choose the intervals of the second line tho it were in the middle of a Batalion which puts them in disorder, and makes them an easie prey to the Enemy that is coming upon them flushed with the victory over the first line, whilst they are so much dampled and discouraged with seeing the first line defeat that they are almost as much in the disposition of running away as it, so that in commonly happens, that that army whose first line is once broke Seldom recovers, but goes with altogether, there is no rule without exception, but that is what happens for the most part, therefore I should think that instead of waiting to remedy the breaking of the first line, till after it has happened which is what is done nowadays since the second line is obliged to stand quietly still till they see the first line defeat before they can so much as attempt to help it, it would be much better to try to prevent its defeat by making the second line support it even in the time of the first attack. It is true that that is impossible in the way the regular forces fight nowadays, As I shall show after this, but tis the easiest thing in the world for the Highlanders to do it, considering the way that they attack, I said at the beginning that the thing that made the attack of the Highlanders so famous, was not only the velocity with which they come in upon the Enemy but also the weight that their joining their strength, by pushing one another gave them against a single rank of the enemy, for tis but a single rank, that they attack at a time, since as the regular forces are obliged to have some distance betwixt them for to have liberty to make use of their Bayonetts, the first rank is broke before they attack the second, I also said that they prevailed most easily in those places where by going unequally towards the Enemy they crowded in in greatest numbers, by consequence the greater number there is to attack in any one place the better, so that if the line was double in number of Ranks or man where they set out it would prevail the more easily by allowing the greater crowd in every particular place, therefore would it not be very easie to order the second line to stand close by the first and never so much as think of shooting but keep their muskets slung over their backs all the time, but when the attack began run in with the first line tho the should be of no more use than to push in the rest, which will make that the foremost man will not only have his own Strength but that of severall others, and will have nothing else to do but justle through and push before him the hedge of bayonets that are in his way, and tho' the being pushed with violence upon the points of bayonets would be a very dangerous situation if he wanted a targe yet by receiving all their points upon his targe he drives them all before him without the least danger, and besides if some of them (which may happen for a wonder) should be shy in attacking so as to want to stop by the way are at least run in more slowly for fear, instead of attacking briskly as they use to do, it would be impossible for him to stop because the crowd coming after him would push him in whether he would or not and after that by such an attack they have so far broke the first line of the Enemy, as to put them to flight, then those that know themselves to be of the second line of the Highlanders may stand still, and while their first line is pursueing the runaways they may draw up in the same order they were in at first to support their first line in case the runaways by getting through the intervals of the second line should allow it to advance in order against the pursuers and repuse them, but if the first line of the Highlanders should drive the runaways so hard as not to allow them to choose the intervals but push them even to the very Batalions, so as to put them in confusion, and by that means get a fair opportunity to attack the second line also to advantage (which I am persuaded will happen for the most part) then the second line of the Highlanders should run in as fast as possible to foreward the second attack as they did the first.

People will say that certainly the Highlanders may strengthen their line by such a practice but may not the regular forces do the same I shall show that if they did do it, it would not only be useless but even disadvantageous and that if they were to put their lines near one another the one to support the other they would make even less resistance that way than the way they commonly are set I mean the second line within three or four hundred yards of the other; In the first place it would be useless to them both in regard of their firing and in regard of the close Engagement, in regard of firing because it is agreed upon every body that tho' the line was composed of never so many ranks yet it is impossible that more than the three or at most four first ranks should fire because if there was more to fire the shot of the hindmost rank would be apt to do more mischief to the foremost rank than even to the Enemy so that all that would be put in any line more than is usual nowadays behoved to be useless.

It would also be useless in regard of the close Engagement because no forces can be said to support and help one another in the litteral sense, but such as have their efforts so far joined as to work at the same lane, what is it as I said before gives the first of the Highlanders that comes up to the Enemy such a Weight and Strength to penetrate into the Enemy's line, but that he not only has his own strength but also, that the second man that comes up behind him by pushing him communicates to him not only his own strength but also all that has been communicate to him by the push of the whole crowd that are coming up behind him and what is it that makes that the regular forces are too little able to resist the effort of so many people joined together tis because they are not joined together nor contigious to one another, but are obliged to stand at some distance from one another to have room to make use of their bayonets, so that every rank stands by it self quite loose and discontiguous from any other, and by consequence can have no additional resistance communicate to it by the rest, tis true that when any of the first Rank are tumbled back upon those of the second Rank people may say that it helps to support them but every body will own that one man being pushed and stumbling back upon an other does more harm to his resistance by the unwieldy way by which he falls upon him than he receives good from his help, and if the two first ranks be push back upon the third it still augments the confusion, but besides tis very well known that if they either tumble on man so far back as to get into the line or even push that man's bayonet so far back upon himself as to get in within the length of the broad sword of him, they make so good use of it, that there is little Resistance after that so that in case to augment the resistance the regular forces, should augment the number of the Ranks in a line, the first ranks would be put in disorder and cut to pieces before the additional ranks came in the play, and then the Confusion would be so great that the length of their guns and bayonets would make them so unweildy that they would still be more useless than at the beginning.

But it will be objected next, that tis little matter what advantage we have over foot, if we be so afraid of horse that the last attack of them will put us to the flight; tis true people say that the Highlanders are afraid of horse, but I do not know wherefore, for I do not remember an example of their having been put to flight by horse except that of the left wing at Sherriffmoor which as I said before is not to be an example because it was not composed of Highlanders; but as tis impossible for any troops that are not accustomed to horse not be a little surprised at them at first I shall not deny but it may be the case of the Highlanders, To which I answer that every body knowes that the foot have a great advantage against them, when they are enough accustomed to them not to take a panick at them, and every body knows that courage is so natural to the Highlanders that I am persuaded it would get the better of the terror of the horse as soon if not sooner in them than many other troops, and in the mean time tis the generall's fault if he does not keep them out of those occasions in which the horse can get the better of them, for what is the thing that distinguishes most a good general from a bad one but that a good General takes care to avoid those occasions wherein the troops he commands may place under a disadvantage and takes care to make use of those in which they have the advantage of the Enemy, and tis the easiest thing in the world for a general that commands Highlanders to do so, for whatever advantage people may conclude from what I have said that they have over foot in the feild yet the thing that they delight most in and that their education and way of living teaches them to do to best purpose is the surprising the Enemy by forced marches and sudden unexpected attacks either in passes or in a dark night, which tho it be never so stormy as equal for them to the best of days and which they would choose the rather to go out in because the badness of the weather would make them be less expected at such a time, and there is so many occasions for such attacks in Hilly Countrys or in inclosed ones that tis the general's own fault if he gives the Enemy what people call a fair meeting in case he be afraid of their cavalery which is the greatest absurdity imaginable either to think of giving or expect to get from an Enemy, for is it not one of the greatest qualitys of a general to seek out all occasions of getting a catch of the Enemy, and does any body think that tho they should neglect taking their advantages the Enemy will not take care to make use of all his and even of those occasions against your self that you have omitted, and yet that was the conduct which our people followed in the year 1715 tho there was a number of occasions in which they might have fought them to great advantage which they took care to neglect and even within a few hundred years of the feild of Battle there is to my certain knowledge a narrow pass which the regular forces were absolutely obliged to go through, that very morning to come to the feild of Battle which I should undertake might be kept by 100 men against a whole army, and which they might either have defended in that shape or allowed the one half or any part to get through it and then attacked them before what was behind could get through to support them that were already past, and by consequence escaped to the attack which is the use that a good General commonly makes of a Defile[1], when he is so lucky as to know of one in the

---

1   A narrow pass or gorge between mountains or hills.

road through which the Enemy is to pass, But even after that hen of only lost an occasion of cutting of a great if not the greatest part of the Enemy but even refused allowance for it when a Gentleman that even had been an officer in the regular forces undertook to do so with 500 Highlanders and with very great probability of succeeding it was when they heard that Argiles army was marching from Sterling to attack them in Perth where they were, it was in time of winter which happened that year to be one of the most rigorous that had been known and a vastly deep storm upon the ground so that they had nothing to go upon but a single track that could not contain two a breast which was beaten firm by the few travelers that past that way and horse could not draw up in any manner of line for if they went to either side of that track they sunk in the snow so deep that they would not be able to get out, so that the second horse could not help the first, which would have given the Highlanders a cheap bargain of them, and as for the regular foot tho they could easier have supported themselves upon the snow, they were so much benummed with cold to which they were unacustomed that they could scarce handle a fire lock, whereas the Highlanders that were to attack them by being accustomed to the hills to travail in all weathers, would have thought so little of the cold that they would have been grateful for action which would have made that one of them would have been able to get the better of their Enemies but if 500 could not do the thing why not send out all the Highlanders which, was the greatest part of the army and make use of the advantage such circumstances would have given to recover a cause that they had ruined by their former mismanagement; but there were advantages that they did not think proper to take and lost the cause upon a foolish maggot of not venturing the men, as if men want to the feild for any other end but to venture upon any reasonable appearance of success and especially the Highlanders who never want themselves to be spared on the contrary they would always wish to be upon action, and nothing discourages them so much as keeping them back, when they are wanting to go on; so that I say tis the General's fault if he does not take opportunitys wherein horse are rendered useless, in case the army be deficient in that; But that scarce can be the case either, for when ever the country rises in arms there is always a proportionable quantity of horse men that we always looked upon as being as good for cavalery in proportion as our foot for tho they have not such strong horses as the regular cavalery this country affording none of that size, yet as they are all gentlemen the courage and resolution with which they obliged in honor to act upon that occasion makes them commonly prevail and in that very unlucky affair of the Sherriffmoor if the left wing was beat for want of cavelery as I said before to support them against that of the Emmy it was not but that there was enough in the army, but that Genral Hamilton instead of allowing them to march as they were drawn up in the morning by his wise command put them in such disorder that they were into a place where they were useless, so that they stood the whole day without drawing the sword, while the Enemy was prevailing for the want of them in the place they should have been in therefore there is no reason to fear that there will be want of cavalery to oppose to that of the Enemy's and if there should there will be no want of opportunity of fighting in places where the calvalery will be of so little use.

The next objection is that tis impossible to keep the Highlanders from plunder and when they have got anything by that way tis impossible to hinder them from going home with it, I shall say for their excuse, in the first place, that tis very hard to keep any army tho they were even regular forces from plundering if they be not regularly paid and when they served entirely by way of volunteers and had no pay but what they brought with them or what they could make by their shifts, tis no wonder if they were obliged to take for their substance what they could not get any other way, but every body knows that the last time they were in arms in the year 1715 where they had a kind of pay tis well known that they almost all behaved a great deal better than the regular troops that came after them even in regards of those people who could not have complained if they had made a little free with their houses, because they were known to be disaffected to the cause, the Highlanders were for, and I am sure that in case of the Highlanders being regularly paid tis the easiest thing in the world to hinder them from plunder, for whatever people may talk of discipline they have amongst them that part of it which regards the authority of Commander over the rest more than any regular troops whatsoever, for there is no Chief amongst them but has a great deal more authority over his men than any Collonel or Commander of the soldiers, and tis very easie for them to do that or any other thing that will be convenient if they choose to be in concert with the General, for there is nothing they cannot get their men to do, And in the year 1715 and several other occasions I know of some acts of authority done by some of the Chiefs particularly in regard or hindering plunder, as no officer in a regular army durst venture upon with his men; and such obedience in the men as no soldiers would pay to their officers; tis true that at the time there were some clans guilty of great disorders in that way, but every body knows it was the faults of their leaders who would not use their authority to hinder it, but we have for the present at the head of the Highlands a set of such pretty Gentlemen, who besides their natural parts and principals of Honour, have for the most part all had the advantage of improving themselves by seeing the world either by travailing after the year 1715 or by a foreign Education, since that there is no doubt but they will come into any Measures to hinder any thing that is either dishonorable to the name of Highlanders or disadvantageous to the cause general, besides as there is no set of men that have more at heart the point of Honour than the meanest amongst the Highlanders have if a General will pike them upon that and will expect things from them more by persuasion than by threats, in fine if he has the way of both making himself esteemed and loved by them, which any good General may do, if he has a way of making himself popular there is no right thing he cannot get them to do and no wrong thing he cannot get them to abstain from.

There is a vast deal more could be said upon the subject which I omitt for fear of being tedious, because it has carried me further already than I intended at first, And the subject is so copious, that I have been obliged for fear of going in to too great a length to restrain myself only to give short hints upon different heads, that I have touched upon, but tis also so plain that I am persuaded if any man reads this and has a thorough knowledge of the art of War especially by experience, the very hints that I have given will bring him into such a feild of Ideas as will easily clear the matter and illustrate the thing to his own satisfaction; there is one thing that I would wish that he should have before his eyes one or more High-landers full armed, for as that is the ground work upon which all that I have said is founded I am persuaded that he would in that case see the thing so clear that it would be very convincing.

Since it is no less certain than a Mathematical Demonstration as I said before and I do not see why it cannot be brought under consideration in a Mathematical way as well as most part of other things; for what is a Man but a machine composed by nature subject to the laws of motion, and governed thereby, And an Armed man afoot is nothing but a complex machine half formed by nature and half formed by art, the half that is formed by nature is the man as aforesaid and the half that is formed by art is the Arms that he carries; A horse man again is a machine composed of a man a horse and arms, what then can people call an army but a great machine, composed of squadrons of horsemen and Batalions of Men afoot, whereof courage is the spring, and the General is the Mechanick that governs the whole, to break down and destroy another great machine of the same kind, that is set up in opposition to it, and all the odds betwixt a Good General and a bad one is, that the bad General knows in general that the machine is to be moved but has neither knowledge of what effect the different parts of the machine nor can fore see what opposition, he may meet with from the machine he works against, and by consequence does not know what parts of his machine to work at proper times, and either lets the machine stand still when it should work, or moves one part of it when another should be imployed and does not know what natural remedy to make use of what he sees that the parts he has made use of do not answer the end he ignorantly expected from them; whereas a good General like a skillful mechanick knows the fort and the foible of every particular part, not only of his machine whatever situation or circumstances they may be imployed in, but also of those parts of the opposite machine he is to work against, and what effect every one part of his, will have against every part of the opposite machine, and takes care to imploy every one of them in those occasions where he thinks the effect he knows they are to produce will prevail most certainly, what then can hinder me from saying that one machine may be better adapted according to the laws of motion to the effect that is intended by those kind of machines, and to show even to as great a demonstration as any other part of Mechanicks can be brought to that a set of Highlanders is the machine that has ever yet been produced that will be most effectual against any other machine or set of troops just now existing and that none are so fit to attack them as they are to resist, and that on the contrary none are so fit to resist as they are to attack; it will be objected to me that there is one part of the Humane machine either in particular or general which I have not spoke of and which is as essential to it, and may give it very unexpected turns quite contrary to the regular effects I expect for it, which is hope and fear, tis very true that the motions of the mind are so uncertain that tis impossible to bring them into such a regular system as those of a body, but I believe that in the case of an army which we are speaking of, these Motions of the mind are commonly equal of both sides, and if there be any difference as they have a great connection with those of the Body and are commonly the consequences of one another, if the Highlanders have the advantage in other things as I think I have showen on the foregoing work and as I am sure they themselves believe the have it is not to be supposed that fear will have much effect upon them but

{Note: In the original manuscript, the page numbered "50" is missing}

in their appearance at a Review and the way they are treated by the Generalls shoes that they look upon them as the troops of the whole Army that do best the duty in a camp, and tho' they have not had any occasion of being tried in the feild of Battle, Yet I dare answer that they will do at least as well as any regular troops can do, but what of that in the way there are in and are ordered to fight with guns & bayonets, they are no better than other regular troops, and tho' in a regular army their courage might make them behave at least as well if not better than their neighbours, and yet I would undertake with an equal number of the clans to fight with and get the better of them as easily as any other regular forces; but if you will return them their targes broad swords and pistolls and by adding some things and returning a great many, from the exercise they have learned you adapt it so far to the Highland way as to make it rather an advantage than a hindrance, I should undertake with that single Batalion not only to engage equal but even double their number of any troops in the world, and should answer to get the better of them under the highest penalty which shows that the Highlanders are probably as good Men as any in the world, yet it is the arms they carry and the way they make use of them against the Enemy that gives them the greatest advantage.

There is a great many more things to be said concerning the Highlanders, that would carry me too great a length to set them down here But I think I have said enough to convince any body of the verity of the propostion I advanced at the beginning if it does not do so I can assure you it is not the fault of the subject treated of but of the dress tis put in by a unskillfull hand, and it is no wonder if the stile be both confused and unpolished since it is the first time I ever put pen to paper for any thing of this kind, and probably will never undertake any thing like it again, and I own I was very unfit and very unequal to task of this kind and that. But really thing appeared to me of such importance that when I saw nobody else like to do it I thought realy that the duty I owe to my King and Country required of me rather to venture to do it wrong than not see it done at all for where is the General that has either Service or experience that will venture his Reputation in any Expedition with troops without knowing how far he may depend upon them? And where is the man or set of men that will venture their lives and fortunes with people without knowing how far these people by their courage and conduct will answer the end that is expected from them, if then by what I have said I can get people to know the real value of the Highlanders and depend upon them.

{Note: Any further pages of the document are missing in the original MS}

JOHN FERDINAND

I n 1788, a printed pamphlet entitled *The Sword's-Man* was published by subscription in Edinburgh, containing "a series of observations on the use of the sword." Although not a lengthy tome as compared to other fencing texts of the period, this succinct little pamphlet treats of the three staple fencing weapons of the era—the broadsword, small-sword, and spadroon. Its concise length may be attributed, in part, to the fact that it is by no means a beginner's text, as the author almost completely ignores the basic technical aspects of fencing—instead, declaring that "the following sheets are, only intended for the use of such as are acquainted with the rudiments of the art of defense" and that it is "well calculated for a Guide to those already versed in the principles of the same Art."

Of the author, John Ferdinand, almost nothing is known beyond what can be found in his little treatise. The sole additional piece of extant evidence that we have been able to find concerning him comes from a page in *Williamson's Edinburgh Directory, from June 1790 to June 1792* (see opposite image). It confirms that John Ferdinand was a fencing master based in Edinburgh, where he ran a school at "Gavinlock's land", a stone building erected by Alexander Gavinlock in 1698, lying on the north side of High Street and opposite the head of Forrester's Wynd—in an area that is now known as the Lawnmarket, in the oldest part of Edinburgh's Old Town.[2]

Aside from this, some additional insight regarding John Ferdinand may be gleaned from the treatise itself. First, in the book's preface, Ferdinand offers his work to the "Nobility and Gentry of Scotland," whom he addresses as "my Lords and Gentlemen." This strongly suggests that Ferdinand either had already cultivated an elite clientele among his fencing students, or that he was extremely bold and presumptuous. Judging by the list of subscribers appended to his treatise, the former would seem to be the likelier case.

Among Ferdinand's subscribers is listed one "Mr Angelo." That such a conspicuous Italian name should appear in a Scottish fencing treatise suggests that it is almost certainly a reference to a member of the illustrious Angelo dynasty of fencing masters. It could possibly refer to the family patriarch, Domenico Tremamando (author of the classic fencing treatise, *L'École des Armes*), or to his son Henry—who took over his father's school in 1785. An even likelier possibility is that the "Mr Angelo" listed therein refers to Domenico's younger brother, John Xavier Angelo, who moved to

---

2   Later, in 1848, Gavinlock's Land was acquired by the Bank of Scotland. *John Knox and the Town Council of Edinburgh: With a Chapter on the So-called "John Knox's House"* (Edinburgh: A. Elliot, 1898), 96-97.

(35)

Fell Thomas, grocer, head of Strichen's clofe
Ferrier James, W.S. George's ftreet
Ferrier Colonel Ilay, Gayfield
Ferrier John, Efq; from Jamaica, Fredrick ftreet
Ferrier & Dallas, importers & dealers in foreign
    wines. & fpiritous liqnors. below Carruber's cl.
Ferrier Robert, wax chandler, Lawnmarket, houfe in
    St. John's ftreet
Ferrier   , fmith & ferrier, Pleafance
Ferie Alexander, writer, Canongate head
Fergus Mrs, No 14, Hanover ftreet
Forgie David, taylor, head of the Pleafance
Ferdinand Daniel, hair dreffer, St. Andrew's ftreet
Ferdinand John, fencing mafter, Gavinlock's land
Ferguffon Walter, Efq; writer, Buchanan's court
Ferguffon George, Efq; adv. No 31. Prince's ftreet
Ferguffon Alex. Efq; advocate, No 16, Hanover ftr.
Ferguffon Niel, Efq; advocate, George's ftreet
Ferguffon James, Efq; of Pitfour, advoc. Luckenb.
Ferguffon Adam, prof. of Moral Philofophy Scienes
Ferguffon Alexander, writer, James's fquare
Ferguffon Will. of Raith No 25 St. Andrew's ftr.
Ferguffon Mifs, of Kilerran, No 7, St. James's fq.
Ferguffon Mrs, room fetter, Chapel ftreet
Ferguffon Alexander, hair dreffer, Rofe ftreet
Ferguffon Mrs, midwife, Parliament clofe
Ferguffon Alex. dyer, Lawnmarket, fouth fide
Ferguffon Walter, candlemaker, Lawn market
Ferguffon Thomas, copperfmith, Weft bow
Ferguffon John, copperfmith, Weft bow
Ferguffon Robert, mafon, Wrights houfes
Ferguffon William, broker, Cowgate port
Fettes William, wine mercht, head Bailie Fyfe's cl.
Fernie William, baker, St Patrick's fquare
Fernie William, baker, Rofe ftreet
Figgans James, folicitor at law, Forefter's wynd
Finch, Weddell & Co. confectioners No 14, S. Br. ft.
Finlayfon William, writer, Writers court
Findlayfon John, grocer, Canongate head
Findlay William, fpirit dealer, Blackfriars wynd
Findlay Hugh, merchant, head Mint clofe
Findlay Mrs, mantuamaker, Meal market ftairs

Edinburgh in 1763, where he established a *manège* and Edinburgh Academy of Exercises (later, in 1766, the Royal Edinburgh Academy of Exercises), and where he served as fencing, riding, and dancing master.[3] The fact that the "Mr Angelo" mentioned by Ferdinand was one of the few subscribers to order "two copies" gives rise to the possibility, of course, that more than one member of the Angelo family was a recipient of *The Sword's-Man*.

Another conspicuous name among Ferdinand's list of subscribers, worth mentioning, is one "John Taylor"—a possible reference to the "Broad Sword Master to the Light Horse Volunteers of London and Westminster," and the author of "Ten Lessons" of the broadsword published in 1799 and again in 1804.[4] Although John Taylor was not an uncommon name of the period, the fact that this broadsword master and author was also directly connected to the Angelo family, as proclaimed in the title of the 1799 *Guards of the Highland Broadsword, as Taught at Mr. H. Angelo's Academy: on the Ancient Scottish Principles Introduced by Mr. Taylor, Broadsword Master to the Light Horse Volunteers of London & Westminster,* is a coincidence too notable to be dismissed.[5]

---

3 This information courtesy of Maestro Paul Macdonald of Edinburgh, and Henry Angelo, *Angelo's Pic Nic* (London: Kegan Paul, Trench, Trübner & Co. Ltd., 1905.), xii, xviii, xxii.

4 *The Guards of the Highland Broadsword, as Taught at Mr. H. Angelo's Academy: on the Ancient Scottish Principles Introduced by Mr. Taylor, Broadsword Master to the Light Horse Volunteers of London & Westminster* ([London], Piccadilly: 1799) *The Art of Defence on Foot, with the broad sword and sabre: adapted also for the spadroon; Augmented with the ten lessons of Mr. John Taylor* (London: T. Egerton, 1804.).

5 Henry Angelo served with John Taylor in the Light Horse Volunteers. A 1799 print *Representing in one View the Manual & the Ten Divisions of the Highland Broad Sword* states that Henry Angelo was "Fencing Master to the Light Horse Volunteers."

Whatever the identity of Ferdinand's subscribers, he makes clear that his text is intended for real action. Among its pages, Ferdinand insists that his text is "void of those flourishes, only intended to divert the curious and ignorant," and writes of his aim

> to treat only of such observations and assaults, as I imagine useful with sword in hand, serving as a guide to those gentlemen who may be under the disagreeable necessity of drawing either to protect life, or defend their injured honour.

He concludes his introductory section by noting that no book can ever replace a master, admonishing other published authors, as well as potential readers who might misunderstand his intentions:

> Several books on this subject, have been offered to the public, to supply the place of a Master; which attempt, in my humble opinion, does no honour to their respective authors...Fencing depends greatly on the exact motions of the body, arms, and legs, which no gentleman can acquire by the directions of a book; it being necessary to practice them in the presence of a teacher, whose attention should be to correct the least defects; for, in the first lessons of that art, depends the good or bad habits of the body, for ever after...My principal motive for this publication, is the thoughts of the necessity of a book on the subject, proper to guide the swords-man in the field, where safety is the chief object, in executing any design.

THE

S W O R D'S - M A N;

CONTAINING

A Series of Observations on the Use of the S W O R D;

IN THREE PARTS.

PART I. Useful Remarks and Lessons respective to the Small Sword	PART II. The Use of the Broad Sword
	PART III. The Use of the Spadroon

THE whole being carefully produced from an attentive Study on the Theory, and Practice of the Art of Defense, is well calculated for a Guide to those already versed in the principles of the Same Art.

BY *JOHN FERDINAND*, TEACHER OF FENCING

EDINBURGH:

PRINTED BY A. ROBERTSON, for the AUTHOR.

M,DCC,LXXXVIII.

PRICE TWO SHILLINGS

TO THE

NOBILITY AND GENTRY

OF

S C O T L A N D.

My LORDS and GENTLEMEN,

PERMIT me to offer to your perusal, the observations contained in this treatise, which I have committed to print, not from a desire of being thought an author, but merely to seek the opportunity of doing myself the honor to sacrifice to you, whatever discoveries I have been able to make in the use of the Sword, fit to put in practice.

I have omitted copper-plates, conceiving them to be more amusing than instructive; especially as the following sheets are, only intended for the use of such as are acquainted with the rudiments of the art of defense.

Several books on this subject, have been offered to the public, to supply the place of a Master; which attempt, in my humble opinion, does no honour to their respective authors.

Fencing

Fencing depends greatly on the exact motions of the body, arms, and legs, which no gentleman can acquire by the directions of a book; it being necessary to practice them in the presence of a teacher, whose attention should be to correct the least defects; for, in the first lessons of that art, depends the good or bad habits of the body, for ever after.

This consideration has induced me to treat only of such observations and assaults, as I imagine useful with sword in hand, serving as a guide to those gentlemen who may be under the disagreeable necessity of drawing either to protect life, or defend their injured honour.

That the whole may afford the desired satisfaction here intended for the amateurs of the system of defense, is the earnest wish, of,

My Lords and

Gentlemen,

Your dutiful humble servant

JOHN FERDINAND.

ADVERTISEMENT.

I have omitted those lessons which are commonly taught at schools, more adapted for amusement than real service.

Such lessons as I treat of are easy, safe, and void of those flourishes, only intended to divert the curious and ignorant.

As to disarms, and passes taught by old Masters, who to this day shew them, because they have been so instructed, when the use of the sword was less refined I should deem myself very ignorant in my profession, and guilty of an insult, was I to offer them to my kind readers.

My principal motive for this publication, is the thoughts of the necessity of a book on the subject, proper to guide the swordsman in the field, where safety is the chief object, in executing any design.

PART I.

In the use of the small sword, you have three different measures to observe in assaulting.

The *First*, is when you or your adversary are not entirely at a distance, to be able to touch by a longe.

The *Second*, when you or him are within reach.

The *Third*, when either of you have retired, and that the other pursues.

When you draw your sword, stand on the first measure, that you may prevent the enemy's surprising you; and thus out of distance, you will discover the nature of his thrusts, if he assaults, and what parades he uses when you attack. In both cases, endeavor to command your body, so as to remain out of reach, till a favourable opportunity offers for the execution of your thrusts.

The keeping an opponent thus at a distance, by not suffering him to approach is point beyond yours, is the fastest method of engaging sword in hand; and not so much exposed to feints and disarms, as the half-sword play used at schools.

Among other cautions in assaulting, observe the following very material ones.

Seem to fear a rash fencer, that you may gain some advantage of him; and attack a timid one briskly, in order to baffle his intentions, and put him in confusion; but, at the same time, observe well the danger of every thrust you may attempt.

When you advance upon your adversary, make only half-thrusts at him to prick his sword-arm, never pushing beyond the lengths of his elbow, unless he gives you a very fair opening. This is the most prudent way of assaulting; and, a few wounds in the hand, wrist, or arm, may have the desired effect.

In your attacks seldom make more than one thrust at the same place, in the same manner; but, after your method as occasion may require.

Should you engage a man much taller than yourself, who depends on keeping you at a distance, by the additional length of his arm, try to bind his sword gently and inclose him, not neglecting to be ready to parry his disengagements at the time of your attempt. If he attacks you, endeavor to inclose him as you parry; for by that you will gain the point of his sword, coming within the reach of a thrust, which he cannot easily defend, his arm being too far advanced to oppose you.

In your attempts against any adversary, if you find yourself exposed by his unexpected maneuver, so that you cannot recover quick enough to come to a parade, spring off with your point well fixed before him ready to oppose, should he follow you.

Sometimes it is very convenient, when within distance, to draw back your left leg as you parry, that the enemy's thrust may not reach you; which affords you a quick repost before he can recover. This is a great deception against the best judges of measure.

When your antagonist longes at you, do not wait for his recovery as the ancients used to do, by which they often lost their reposts, for the opponent, by remaining on the longe, resting on the right leg, would bring imperceptibly the left closer to it, and by that artful motion come to his guard, before the other could throw in his thrust; so that as soon as you parry, from your repost with an extention while your adversary is on the longe, for if you also longe out at the same time, both meeting too near; your point will often miss his body, as you cannot make a good opposition; but should you find him too far off in the attempt of his thrust, by his not having judged his distance properly; then in that case, you are to take what longe becomes necessary for your repost.

When your antagonist keeps you guarded with the point high, and the wrist somewhat low, you may use the feints of one, two; one, two, three in quarte, or in quarte over the arm, or cut over the point.

If he thrusts or feints at you with the point high and the wrist low, you may use simple parades, as his feints become very slow, and will often afford you a good repost from your simple parades.

Should he on the contrary, hold his blade horizontal, you may use the round parades of quarte, and tierce with the circle.

The quarte guard, with your wrist breast high, is on the safest to stand an assault; and though the lower part of your body may be exposed, yet you have it in your power, by the dropping of your point, to come to demicircle, octave or sixieme; which cannot be done when low guarded, without exposing the upper part of your body in forming such parades, or be too late in executing them, should you rise your sword-hand when your enemy's thrusts come under your wrist.

When guarded in quarte, you are to depend on the parade of round quarte, to protect yourself from your opponent's disengagements over your arm; and the parade of demicircle to defend those attempted under your wrist. These are the best parades used with the small-sword, which by doubling as may be found necessary, will, with the help of octave now and then, readily answer your antagonist's deceptions.

In opposing the disengagements over the arm, and under your wrist, you may use five ways:

First, with double round quarte. *Second*, with one round quarte and tierce. *Third*, with one round quarte and demicircle. *Fourth*, with one round quarte and sixieme. *Fifth*, with one round quarte and octave.

The *first* and *second* serve to parry the attempts made over the arm. *Third, fourth,* and *fifth* to oppose those under and above the wrist.

If you, by being used to it, prefer the guard of quarte over the arm; depend chiefly on the parades of quarte, demicircle, prime, and round tierce; though this last parade is often failable, when attacked by a quick fencer, while within due measure; but is of excellent use to disarm if a little out of distance.

To oppose your antagonist's attempts made inside of your sword-arm, and those under your wrist, you can practice the following five:

First, one round tierce, and simple quarte. *Second,* a double round tierce. *Third,* one round tierce, and demicircle. *Fourth,* one round tierce and octave. *Fifth,* one round tierce and sixieme.

The *first* and *second* serve to parry the disengagements made at you in quarte. The *third, fourth,* and *fifth,* those above and under your wrist.

The guards or tierce, prime, sixieme octave and demicircle; though used by many, are, in my humble opinion, very open and weak to receive the attack; and only proper to use according to the changes of the enemy's thrusts.

When you parry with simple or round tierce, you can use the reposts of tierce and segonde; or the feints of segonde to touch in quarte over the arm; or those of segonde, quarte over the arm to hit in segonde.

Should you parry any thrust over the arm with round quarte, you may repost quarte and flanconade; or feint quarte to touch in quarte over the arm or feint flanconade to thrust quarte.

If you parry with demicircle, you can repost either high or low quarte, or feint low quarte, to touch in quinte.

When you parry with prime, repost cave; which is a thrust in the quarte side, with the wrist in the position of tierce. You may also feint cave, and thrust segonde.

Observe that whenever you parry prime and repost cave, you must bring your left toes close to your right heel, and oppose your left-hand to the enemy's blade, by which you thin your body and escape his point that was in the line and reposted, he might have advanced his arm and touched you through revenge, though himself endangered by your point. Some advance both feet when they parry prime, to pass the adversary's point, that they may repost safely.

If you parry with octave repost quinte, or feint the same, or thrust high or low quarte.

Should you parry with sixieme, repost quarte, quarte over the arm; or feint quarte over the arm to touch in segonde; or feint quarte over the arm, feint segonde to hit in quarte over the arm.

ASSAULTS.

ON THE FIRST MEASURE

I.

On guard in quarte, your adversary marches upon you in the same quarte, to gain measure; as soon as he comes within distance, cross his blade, and thrust flanconade.

II.

On guard in quarte, your antagonist advances upon you in the quarte side, fix your point well in the position of the thrust of quarte, and bring your left toes close to your right heel, by which his point passes you and yours touches him. The motions of the hand and foot must be joined in one, by moving both parts of the body at the same time. In these kind of voltings, it is very prudent to oppose the left hand to the enemy's blade. Such a manner of breaking the line, is very convenient when engaged with a rash fencer.

III.

On guard in quarte, your antagonist advances upon you in quarte, as soon as he comes within distance, whip on his blade in the quarte side and enter quarte; if he opposes your stroke with quarte, push quarte over the arm. You must be careful when you whip on the blade, not to throw your arm so much out of the line, as to disable you to come to a parade, should you miss the blade by your antagonist's deceiving you with a disengagement, at the time you attempted to strike it.

IV.

On guard in quarte, your adversary marches changing in quarte over the arm; immediately on perceiving him within distance, whip on his quarte over the arm, with the inside edge of your blade, and enter quarte over the arm; if he opposes you with back quarte or tierce, disengage and thrust quarte.

V.

On guard in quarte, your adversary advances changing in quarte over the arm; you thrust quinte or segonde, on his coming within measure.

On guard in quarte over the arm, your antagonist, marches on you with the same, holding his point high and his wrist low; advance a step upon him at the time, raising your arm, fixed in the position of a thrust, and throw forward quarte over the arm, which, if properly delivered, guards you and enters without opposition.

ASSAULTS.

ON THE SECOND MEASURE

I.

On guard in quarte over the arm, give a small opening, that low quarte may be pushed at you; which if done, parry with demi-circle, and repost quarte.

II.

On guarde in quarte over the arm, inviting your adversary to throw quarte, which as soon as he does, parry with prime, advancing at the same time, so that you may pass his point, and quickly repost cave.

III.

You and your antagonist being engaged in quarte, bear upon his blade, that he may thrust quarte over the arm, on your perceiving it, parry with round quarte, and enter flanconade.

IV.

On guard in quarte over the arm, press a little on your antago-nist's blade; if he disengages quarte, meet his demicircle, bind his blade and whirl yours round him till you come to the opening, which this gives you over his arm, and thrust a quarte over the arm, which must be done without ever quitting his blade.

V.

On guard in quarte over the arm, your adversary thrusts quinte at you, parry him with octave, bringing him to quarte, repost quarte with your nails well turned up.

VI.

On guard in quarte, your antagonist thrusts quarte over the arm, parry him with round quarte, and crossing his blade quickly with a jerk, you will form a good disarm.

ASSAULTS.

ON THE THIRD MEASURE

I.

Having, (I will suppose) engaged your adversary in quarte, that you find him guarded in quarte with his point high, and the wrist low, and that you feint quarte over the arm, to touch him with high or low quarte, and he upon your feint retires parrying simple tierce, desirous of being pursued, to effect his lurches; you must then disengage quarte, bringing your left foot close to your right; and though he may again have retired on your first disengagement, yet the closing of the left foot to your right, brings you within reach of a longe: This is termed stealing measure.

II.

Engage your enemy in quarte, bear a little upon his blade; should he oppose your pressing, disengage quarte over the arm; if he retires parrying round quarte, bear again upon his blade as soon as he brings you to a quarte, raising your left leg at the same time from your longe, and quickly thrust simple or double quarte over the arm: The bringing up the left leg, is a great deception against those who keep retiring as they parry.

III.

On guard in quarte over arm with your antagonist, advance upon him in quarte, advance again in quarte over the arm and thrust segonde; this is a good attack on a person that uses the simple parades.

IV.

March upon your antagonist in quarte over the arm, as soon as he comes to meet you with the parade of round quarte, draw back your arm a little to escape his blade, and quickly throw quarte over the arm, which is a great deception against the parade of round quarte.

V.

Advance on your adversary in quarte, he retires without opposition, cross his sword with a jerk and thrust tierce or segonde; which if it does not disarm, will give you a sufficient opening for a thrust.

VI.

March upon your enemy in tierce, he keeps retiring with his point high, opposing you in tierce, turn your wrist in quarte, and raising your arm well, slanting your point, push quarte over the arm, without quitting the blade.

VII.

Advance upon your antagonist disengaging in quarte over the arm, and throwing yourself out of the line, by bringing your left toes opposite to your right heel, and immediately disengage and thrust quarte, which is a good deception when simply parried in tierce.

VIII.

March upon your adversary in quarte over the arm, and coming within distance, batter on the same side by hitting his blade within two inches of the point, and sustaining your stroke well upon a slant; thus you will either disarm him, or gain an opening to hit him with a quarte over the arm.

IX.

Advance on your adversary in quarte over the arm, feint a cut over the point in quarte, and disengage a quarte over the arm, under and close to his shell; or, to deceive your adversary's parade, feint a cut over the point in quarte, make another feint of a cut there, by raising your blade a little, and disengage a quarte over the arm.

X.

March upon your opponent in quarte, binding his blade gently till you have gained his point, and drop yours under, and inside of his wrist, and thrust there. This often succeeds if you are active; but be careful to oppose any disengagement from the enemy, at the time you advance with your binding.

XI.

Advance upon adversary in low quarte, he opposes you with demicircle, upon which you immediately raise your wrist a little, and with the inside-edge of your blade, batter strongly upon the flat and foible of his blade, which forms the best disarm that can be performed with the small sword; but you must be careful not to raise your wrist too high, nor part from the first line on which you elevated it.

XII.

March upon your antagonist in quarte; make a half thrust of quarte over the arm at him, he parries you with tierce, and advances upon you at the same time to hit you with segonde, then spring or bend your body as far back as that your blade may be disengaged without contracting your arm, or moving your feet, and thrust quarte.

THE END OF THE FIRST PART.

THE

SWORD'S MAN

PART SECOND.

THE USE OF THE

BROAD SWORD.

In executing any cut with the broad sword, you should seldom or never longe fully out, as taught by many; for when a person is on a full longe, his right leg may be cut, as he cannot easily recover; therefore, half longes and cuts from an extention are the fastest, and the quickest thrown in.

Cuts attempted at the head, face, or right leg, should be performed with great caution, as your sword-arm must be advanced to execute such designs; and may be cut by the enemy, whole blade must often touch you before yours can hit those parts of the body; his sword being nearer your arm, that yours to the parts mentioned. The cuts at the outside of the wrist are very good, and attended with less danger than any other.

As the cuts of the broad sword are made by disengagements over the point, you must take great care in disengaging very narrow; and remember that every disengagement over the point is, much exposed to time, cuts and thrusts.

When you engage with the broad sword, never keep your point higher than your enemy's head; and observe generally to have the wrist low, to prevent the surprise of a cut there.

You must be very careful in having your right leg ready to slip from any cut, which often affords you a good repost at the adversary's head or arm.

The inventors of the use of the broad sword, only introduced five guards, four of which to defend the whole body, and one merely to cut from. But practice having covinced me, that the use of an inside hanging guard somewhat in the form of prime, is of excellent service to defend the cuts thrown inside of the body, I recommend it to you in serious matters, as a very fine parade, which will also afford you a good repost with a medium at the head.

Traversing is of great service; for in keeping within a circle, no body can inclose you to any disadvantageous place; it being in your power to march and retire in the same circle, as long as you find it convenient; and though your enemy may not chuse to traverse, yet you can force him to it, by keeping round, which will induce him to face you, in order to defend himself.

ASSAULTS.

I.

If you are on an outside guard, and that your adversary throws a cut at the inside of your body, parry with an inside guard, and advance a little as you defend, then quickly turning your hand into an outside guard, draw your edge along the right side of his face, and spring off.

II.

If you should be on an inside guard, and that your antagonist throws at the outside of your face, defend his cut with an outside advancing at the same time; and turn up your nails in the form of an inside guard, drawing your edge along his face as you fly off.

III.

On guard on an outside, feint inside of your adversary's leg with half a cut, which gives him an opportunity to throw at your head, and if he does, be ready to parry with St. George, and repost on the outside of his leg.

IV.

On guard on an outside, feint an outside of the thigh, feint at the head, and throw inside of the leg.

V.

On guard on an inside, feint inside of the wrist, and throw outside of the arm.

VI.

Suppose your enemy lays his leg to be cut at, with an intention to slip it, and touch you on the head or arm; as soon as you perceive it, bend your body back and let his blade fall, when immediately cut outside of his arm, leg, or at his head.

VII.

On guard on an outside with your point lower than your wrist, and your arm extended, if your antagonist cuts at the outside of your basket, somewhat turned outwardly, which brings part of your blade upon his arm, and the drawing of it to you, will form a good cut.

VIII.

Stand guarded with a low inside, holding up at the bottom of your basket, and the point downwards, inclining still to an inside guard; this not being very customary, will be thought a very awkward position, and therefore induce your antagonist to cut at the outside of your wrist or arm, upon which turn your basket, and swing your point to an inside upon him at the same time, on the outside of the arm or face.

IX.

You and your antagonist being now traversing to the right or left, he raises his arm to throw a medium at you, upon which you quickly hit him with an inside blow, between the wrist and the elbow, on the time, and double an outside upon traversing to the left.

X.

On guard on an outside, your adversary feints inside and outside, and throws inside of your face; oppose him with an inside guard, and whirl him to a hanging guard, which will either disarm him or gain an opening for a cut at the outside of his face.

XI.

Advance upon your antagonist well covered with a medium, feint outside of his face; as soon as he turns his weapon to defend himself, you must quickly disengage, and cut at his head with a medium; but you are to be careful in executing this cut, as the success of it depends much upon activity, for it is to be done while he turns his wrist. If he should not answer your feint at the outside of the face, cut on the outside of the arm; observing, that in both cases, you must fly off on delivering the cut.

XII.

Stand on a hanging guard, your adversary throws a medium at your head, parry with St. George, feint a medium, and cut at the inside of his face under his point, and double it outside of his arm, then drop your blade, so that he may be tempted to throw at your head, which you must defend by partly sinking your head, and partly raising your arm, and immediately strike at the outside of his leg.

THE END OF THE SECOND PART.

THE

SWORD'S MAN

PART THIRD.

———

THE USE OF THE

SPADROON.

The spadroon being a sword properly edged and pointed to cut and thrust; you naturally have a double advantage with it, either against a small sword or broad sword-player.

With this kind of weapon, you can use both the parades, thrusts and cuts of the small and broad sword, as occasion may require; observing that the true knowledge of the spadroon, consists in severally joining, or separately playing the lessons of the small or broad sword.

A S S A U L T S.

I.

Stand on an outside guard, your adversary feints thrusts or cuts at the outside of your body, oppose him with a round quarte, make half-thrusts in quarte, and fly off with a drawing cut inside his wrist.

II.

On guard in quarte, your antagonist advances joining you with an inside guard, immediately disengage a quarte over the arm as you will find an opening for it; if he parries you with tierce, fly off cutting at the inside of his wrist, or outside of his thigh or leg.

III.

On guard in quarte, your antagonist joins your blade with an outside guard, you quickly raise your arm and thrust quarte over, or under the arm; if he traverses to the left, that you may miss him to cut outside of your leg, you must slip it, and cut at his head.

IV.

On guard in quarte over the arm, make a half thrust in quarte, as soon as your antagonist opposes you with a quarte, disengage over his point, and feint a cut at the outside of his right arm, which he will naturally defend; but whether he does, or does not, thrust segonde, or throw a cut at the outside of his leg.

V.

Stand on guard on an inside, your antagonist disengages quarte over the arm at you, parry with tierce, and close the left foot to the right, at the same time that you may catch him with segonde.

VI.

On guard in quarte over the arm, your adversary feints an inside cut at your face, expecting you to throw a time thrust right forward; and as soon as you do it, he parries you with a whip in quarte, to enter cave; this you must oppose with a prime, and cut with a medium at his head, if he defends with St. George, draw your body back, hold your feet still, and step in cave; then recover in quarte, and wrench into a segonde, enter segonde, or cut outside the arm, as you fly off.

VII.

On guard on an outside, feint with an inside cut at your adversary's face, feint inside of his wrist, and quickly thrust quarte over the arm.

VIII.

On guard in tierce, feint segonde, feint tierce, bringing your right heel at the same time opposite to your left toes, and disengage a cut at the inside of your antagonist's leg, in throwing yourself thus out of the line, you save your head and arm from the enemy's blade which was on the same line with yours, and might have offended you on the time.

IX.

Now stand on a hanging guard well covered, and your point stretched out make a feint of any thrust at your adversary, face, and guard on yourself immediately with St. George, if he takes this opening and cuts at your leg, slip it quickly and return a blow at his head or arm.

X.

On guard in quarte, disengage over the enemy's point, with the feint of a cut at the outside of his arm, then immediately disengage half a thrust under his shell in quarte, and finish the thrust in quarte over the arm.

XI.

On guard in an outside, feint inside and outside of the face. And make a half cut at the outside of the leg, ready to parry with St. George, should your adversary take this opening by slipping his leg to throw a medium at your head, and as you parry with St. George, feint cave and draw back your arm a little in the position of a medium, when quickly cut at the outside of his arm.

XII.

On guard with an inside guard somewhat in form of prime your antagonist cuts at the outside of your wrist or along your right side, immediately raise your point and fix yourself in tierce, with the wrist low, and repost a cut at his head or thrust segonde. Remember to slip the right leg as you parry, for fear his cut should fall low, and escape the parade which you form.

FINIS.

A

L I S T

O F   T H E

S U B S C R I B E R S   N A M E S.

A.	Copies	D.	
Anderson, William Mr	2	D'Asti, Theodore,	
Angelo, Mr	2	Duff, Hugh, Esq;	
Abercromby, John, Esq;		Douglas, A. Esq;	
B.		Douglas, J. Esq;	
Baillie, S. James, Esq;		Dalrymple, John,	
Bruce, Barnet, Esq;		E.	
Busseby, J. H. Esq;		Erskine, Henry, Esq;	
Bewer, John, Esq;		F.	
C.		Fraser, Patrick, Mr	2
Crawford, John, Mr		Forbes, Anthony	
Corbet, John, Mr		Forest, John, Mr	
Cunningham, Alexander		G.	
Cunningham, Thomas		Gibbons, Mr	
Cunningham, J. Esq;		Grant, Robert, Esq;	
Campbell, Duncan, Esq;		H.	
Colden, A. Esq;		Harrison, Thomas,	
Churchill, Charles, Esq;		Hunter, R. Esq;	
Campbell, John, Esq;		J.	
Cochrane, James, Esq;		Jamieson, John, Esq;	
M'Callen, Doctor.		L.	
		Lamond, John, Mr	

Lebon, Archibald, Esq;

M.

M'Donald, Esq;

M'Donell, Milles, Esq;

Maitland, Charles, Esq;

Macallum, William, Mr

M'Kencie, George, Esq;

Mills, John, Esq;

Murray, Patrick, Esq;

Murray, George, Esq;

Miller, William, Esq;

Maxwell, Patrick, Esq;

Miller. P. Esq;

O.

Oliphant, J. S. Esq;

Oliphant, L. Esq;

P.

Ponton, Andrew, Doctor

R.

Richardson, Jacob,

Rsdhrad [sic] Joseph,

Ross, Mr

S.

Smull, Thomas, Mr

Sharp, A. Esq;

Steel, Esq;

Short, James Esq;

de St. Saphorin, Esq;

S.

Thompson, William,   2

Thompson, John, Mr

Taylor, John, Mr

W.

Walker, Esq;   2

Westen, Martin, Esq;

HARY FERGUSSON

In July of 1774, a small notice appeared in Edinburgh's *Caledonian Mercury*, announcing the availability of a "A DICTIONARY, Explaining the terms, guards, and positions, used in the art of the Small Sword."[6] This thin octavo volume, which had been published several years earlier in 1767 would, more than a century later, draw the notice of fencing scholar Carl Thimm, who listed it in his massive *Complete Bibliography of the Art of Fence.*[7] A nineteenth century author described it thus:

> The various explanations of this little fencing dictionary, are concise and explicit; and, doubtless, of value to all who study the so-called noble art.[8]

---

6   *Caledonian Mercury*, Saturday, July 9, 1774.

7   Carl Albert Thimm, *A Complete Bibliography of the Art of Fence* (London: Franz Thimm & Company, 1891), 60.

8   Alexander Balloch Grosart, *The Works of Robert Fergusson* (London : A. Fullerton, [1851]), ciii.

Indeed, a thorough reading of the *Dictionary* reveals it to be much more than a mere collection of definitions. Embedded within are numerous fencing instructions and technical directions to the reader, thus rendering the text a source of insight into the methods of fencing taught and practiced in late eighteenth century Scotland. Since the time of its publication, however, this most interesting text—a worthy contribution to the fencing literature of the eighteenth century—has more or less disappeared into obscurity.

The book was the work of one Hary Fergusson, an itinerant fencing instructor and Aberdeen native—who, after teaching in Edinburgh for a time, became a soldier, went to sea, and traveled to America, where he became swept up in the events relating to the country's War of Independence. And of Hary and his life we would know virtually nothing more, were it not for the fact that his younger brother, Robert, later attained renown as one of Scotland's best-loved poets—drawing the attention of numerous scholars and historians to the Fergusson family and its origins.

Hary, or Henry, the fencer, was born in Aberdeen in 1742, the eldest of six siblings, which included two brothers (one of which, John, died in infancy) and three sisters. Hary's mother, Elizabeth, was the youngest daughter of John Forbes, a man of agricultural position in Aberdeenshire, and a cadet of the house of Tolquhon. Hary's father, William Fergusson, was an Aberdeenshire clerk, who—while Hary was still a young child—brought his family to Edinburgh's Old Town in search of "improved fortune." There, according to one historian, the family lived in

> A small old house, much smaller than the rest, in the Cap-and-Feather close, a confined alley, memorable in Scottish story, which stood immediately above (the present) Halkerston's Wynd, but whose site is now, it is believed, (from improvements which, in these utilitarian days, only Antiquaries lament,) occupied by North Bridge Street.

ROBERT FERGUSSON.

From a Photogravure by W. Drummond Young, from the Painting by Alexander Runciman in the Scottish National Portrait Gallery. By permission.

Above: Hary's brother, as reproduced in the Poetical Works of Robert Fergusson.

In spite of such humble beginnings, in a letter to a friend, Hary humorously claimed a royal lineage, stating that "I am the son of the ancient, the royal Fergus"—to which his friend responded, "I am heartily glad to hear that ye son of the brave and antient Fergus [is] well."[9]

Hary's younger brother, Robert, was well-educated—having attended grammar school in Dundee, as well as the University of Edinburgh and St. Andrews University—and it is reasonable to assume that Hary, as the eldest sibling, would have received an at least comparable education.[10] In one surviving letter, Hary actually "counseled" Robert in his poetic studies, and provided suggestions regarding the written work of the great future poet. He wrote:

> The former [work] I approve of; but cannot recommend ye latter in point of rhyme. You'll please notice that the first and fifth, and the second and fourth lines in compositions of the like kind, such as Habbie Simson, &c., chime with one another.[11]

Although we do not know from whom he received his fencing instruction, Hary, in a 1773 letter to his mother, asked to be "kindly remember'd to" Mr. John Addison, a man "practised with much reputation in Edinburgh, in the double capacity of music-master, and fencing-master."[12] We do know, judging from comments made in the preface to his *Dictionary*, that Hary Fergusson taught fencing for a time in Scotland—most likely in Edinburgh—prior to the publication of his book.

In 1767, William Fergusson, the family patriarch, died, and the very same year, Hary published his fencing *Dictionary*. The family

---

9   Grossart, xxvi.

10 Alexander Campbell, in *Introduction to the History of Poetry in Scotland* (1798) 288-300.

11 Grossart, lx.

12 Grosart, cvii.

was in great want of money, forcing the boys' mother to rent their home out to lodgers, and their brother Robert (the poet) to begin work as a copyist for the Commissary Office. The next year, in 1768, Hary himself became a mariner and went to sea. A series of letters, written by Hary while abroad and sent home to Edinburgh, provides a record of his travels, as well as a rare and fascinating firsthand account of the career and experiences of an eighteenth century Scottish fencing instructor.

The first such surviving letter was written to his mother, immediately after his first setting out, while still in Scotland:

I. HENRY FERGUSSON TO MRS. FERGUSSON.

Kirkwall Road, 13th May, 1768.
D[ea]r Mother.

After an agreeable passage, I arrived here on Wednesday last, having not been in the least sea-sick. I was on shore yesterday, and had an inclination to buy some tea for you, but that article is at present as dear here as in Edinburgh. If we go for Shetland, shall buy some there, as they tell me it is at no higher a price than 3s. p. pound. The manner of living here agrees with me very well. Yesterday I dined for the first time on salted pork, and made as hearty a meal of it as ever I did in my life. If R[obert] is at home, desire him to cause the St. Andrews carrier to leave any word or letter, at Mrs. Currie's, on the [torn away] for me, as she will forward it to Leith Road. Boats belonging to the ship go ashore every day. I have received about 20s. for foils, with which I have bought two cotton check shirts and a pair of shoes which were too little for my comrade and exactly fitted me. We are uncertain how long our stay may be, therefore, whatever you have to say must be deferred till we come to Cromarty, where we will stay to take in beer, and from [that] place I shall write you. Beef sells here at 1 ½ d.

p. pound, and 14 eggs for a penny. Shall be glad this finds you free
of trouble with respect to necessitous circumstances, and accordingly,

I ever am, D[ea]r Mother,

Yours affectionately,

Hary Fergusson.

Compts to sister, her husband, and family, &c,

The letter was addressed to "Mrs. Fergusson, in Jamieson's Land,
Bell's Wynd, Edinburgh," and it was to this "lowly domicile,"
according to historians, that Hary's brother Robert had returned
from St. Andrews only months before. The next letter by Hary
which has been preserved was written from Plymouth, and indi-
cates that he had recently left his ship, the *Augusta,* for another. It
also gives an account of Hary's struggles to procure income as a
fencing instructor:

II. HENRY FERGUSSON TO MRS. FERGUSSON.

Salisbury at Plymouth, 4th Aug., 1770.

My Dear Mother,

You have the greatest reason of any mother living to call a son's
ingratitude in question, both on account of my bad behaviour
towards you when living together, and my long silence since our
separation. On the 18th of April, the day of Wilkie's enlargement, I
was seized with the fever and ague; on the 3d May I was sent to
Rochester Hospital, where I staid till discharged in the beginning of
June. After coming on board, I relapsed and was very dangerously
ill, but, thanks to God, and the good attendance of the surgeons, I
recovered, and am now as well as ever I was since the moment I
existed. You will easily perceive by the date of this [that] I have left
the Augusta, but thank God the change is for the better. When this
ship was put in commission, I was advised by some friends to apply

to go out in her as master-at-arms; this I could not then do, being so very bad [ill], but about the beginning of last month, as I was then able to crawl up and down, I applied, and though there were upwards of thirty candidates, carried my point, having strong recommendations, but, above all, on account of my knowledge of the sword, which has procured me bread here, when many Scots clerks were starving. The ship is to sail to-morrow for the Halifax station in North America, where, and on the passage, we shall be twixt three and four years from England. As we carry both a commodore and captain, the berth I enjoy is upon that account more lucrative than when only the latter goes. The last master-at-arms in the commodore ship, on that station made an immense sum by being provost-martial at trials; with that chance (my pay p. annum) and fencing dues I shall be able to lay up a good deal of money.

Never [knew] I, what real motherly affection was, till I fell sick, having been obliged to lay out every farthing I had for extra cordials, &c, but these are of little service when compared to the real advantages that flow from the mother's attendance. D[ea]r mother, the climate where we are bound for is so remarkably cold, that I was obliged to buy things suitable to it from top to toe, every article being three prices in that part of the world, and this took up all the trifle I had. I assure you, I am now as careful as formerly I was lavish, having nothing more at heart than to contribute to the maintenance of you at my return. Make my best respects to Mr. and Mrs. Inverarity, to Rob, Peggy, Nan Colly, old Scoroble, John Parker and spouse, &c, &c.

I am, D[ea]r Mother,
Your loving Son,
Hy. Fergusson.

P. S. — Yesterday in the morning a most melancholy accident happened on board this ship. As one of the mariners was playing with his piece, it went off and killed a Glasgow lad of the same corps, who sate directly opposite to him. The half of his head was shot away and his brains scattered about the deck in a most shocking manner: what is very remarkable, the principal person is from the Hulks [?] in Kdy parish, and is called Grierson.

Don't write until you hear again from me, as it is yet uncertain whether we go to Halifax or Boston.

Fergusson's next letter was penned from America, in the ship *Tartar*, which was stationed in the Rapahannock River, Virginia. It was addressed to his brother Robert, in response to an earlier piece of correspondence sent by the latter. Hary's letter is dated October 8, 1773, and gives news of his attempts to teach the use of the small sword in America:

III. HENRY FERGUSSON TO ROBERT FERGUSSON.

D[ea]r Robt.

Since the beginning of last month, when I was favoured with yours of the 1st Feby 1773, I have been in most rivers in this Province and Maryland. Our business was to look out after smugglers; and had we been as active in that duty as others on the American station, I might have been enabled to make my appearance in a brilliant manner: but alas! only a sloop of 80 tons from the West Indies, loaden with coffee and sugar, fell to our lot. I had 16 dollars for my share, 3 of which I gave towards buying a Tender, and every foremast man paid one. The Tender is now mann'd, arm'd, and cruizing Chesapeak Bay, and I am convinced cannot fail of taking prizes; if the officers appointed for that duty are attentive.

We had the most severe winter at Halifax ever experienced in that country. The harbour, though 3 miles across, was frozen over for three weeks; the ship's company walk'd aboard and ashore, nay, all our provisions were got aboard on the ice (which in many places was 36 ft in thickness), notwithstanding the strong N.W. winds which blow most of the winter. When we arrived at Boston we were ordered to this country, which has been as hot this summer as the former was cold in winter. Such a change of climate could not fail to create sickness in the ship's company: but, thank God, only three have died, one a natural death, and the other two drown'd. I had a very severe fitt of sickness at our first coming here; but being so much given to sweating it proved an effectual cure, although I am very weak through that means. I never lived so badly, as aboard here, in point of provisions, every species being the worst of their kinds, and neither butter nor flour to be had.

I desire you will write by the pacquet on receipt, for if you lay hold of any other opportunity, your letter will be too late; the ship being positively ordered home early next spring, to my great satisfaction, being quite tired of a life that my past follies drove me to, and to which I have served too long an apprenticeship. If every thing does not succeed to my expectations, on my arrival in England, I am fully bent to return and settle in this country; having had the fairest offers imaginable, could my discharge have been procured. In Virginia and Maryland in particular, I could do best by acting in a double capacity, by learning [teaching] the small sword, and the exercise of the small arms, there being no regular forces in either province, and the officers of the militia being quite ignorant themselves of that part of their duty.

I desire it as a favour, [that] you would often examine your poetical pieces before you commit them to the press: this advice I hope you'll the more readily take, as most young authors are apt to be more criticized than those who have had a little experience. Pope himself was one of the most careful in this respect, and none yet has ever surpass'd him. When I arrive in England, I shall give you the necessary directions how to send your works, and make no doubt of selling them to advantage, when the ship is paid off.

I am sorry to hear of J. Wright's death: he was a worthy young lad, and one I had a true regard for.

Thick Peter I hope by this time is recovered. I should be glad to hear of Robertson and Addison's success: the latter, if in Edinb[urgh], I desire to be kindly remember'd to. I should also be happy to hear how Sandie Young and John Coomans do, having experienced their kindness, and been happy in their company. In our passage from Boston to Hampton, we had a very narrow escape for [with] our lives, being surrounded with one of the largest water-spouts ever seen, which black'ned the sky for some leagues, and, had we not barely weather'd it, would have sunk the ship and every soul aboard.

Remember me in the strongest manner to my mother, Peggy, [Inve]rarities, Father Parker, &c. &c. If you want to either succeed, or gain esteem, be very careful of what company you keep: this advice I hope you'll take, as it comes from one who has lost himself merely through inattention in that respect. Believe me, it is impossible to write you as I would chuse, being invironed with twenty thousand noisy plagues, not to mention execrations so horrid, that [they] would make the greatest blackguard in Edin[burgh]'s hair stand erect. I hope you'll make it your particular care to study such branches of education as may prove most conducive to your future happiness, and appear at least once every

Sunday in church (I mean the Church of Scotland), for how can you spend your time better? I was, like many, fond of the Church of England's forms, &c. &c, but having been in many Romish Churches since, find these forms are merely the...of laziness, and differ but very little from one another: this you can be convinced of, in perusing a Romish mass-book in English.

I am, with greatest regard,

D[ea]r Rob, your affectionate B[rothe]r,

Hary Fergusson.

P. S. — Direct for me on board the Tartar, Hampton Road, Virginia.

Robert's letter of February, 1773, was the last which Hary would received from the poet. In 1774, after suffering from depression, falling down a flight of stairs in Edinburgh, and injuring his head, Robert was committed into Edinburgh's Darien House, where, in a matter of weeks, he died suddenly at age twenty-four. The next letter to reach Hary from Scotland included the news of his brother's death. He wrote to his mother as follows:

IV. HENRY FERGUSSON TO MRS. FERGUSSON.

Tartar in Halifax Harbour, 6th May, 1775.
D[ea]r Mother,

I received your letter of the 29th October last, containing the very disagreeable news of my brother's death, and acquainting me of Peggy's being married to one Mr. Alexander Duval who, you say, is in a very good way, but the particular branch of business he follows you forgot to mention. It is beyond the power of human invention to describe how I was affected by the loss of an only brother, who always had my interest at heart, and with whom I was yet in hopes to have spent many agreeable days. But that there is no certainty on this side the grave is a truth that we daily experience, and plainly proves that to repine is weakness in the highest degree. I earnestly desire you'll take care of all the papers and writings as he left [a seaman's phrase] for my perusal, for I shall be more pleas'd in being possess'd of them than riches, as the former may serve to perpetuate the memory which the latter can never do.

We are now actually at war with the Americans. A skirmish happen'd at a place ca [torn away] on the 18th ult°. betwixt the Provincials or rebels and [torn away] Majesty's... by... overpowered... after they had burnt two magazines of the enemies stores, [?] obliged to retreat 15 or 18 miles through an incessant fire from behind the stone walls and breaches on the roadside. No certain account of the loss on either side has as yet been published, but the rebels, it is said, have sustained treble the loss of the army. Both camps are so near that the sentries of each army can discourse together on their posts, and the rebels augment daily. Several places have lately been burnt by the army; and it is expected by this, that the town of Marblehead is reduced to ashes. No fresh provisions are to be had for any price in New England, and an entire stop is put to all trade. We are ordered here as a safeguard over the dockyard, where we do duty for fear of the disaffected attempting to set it on fire. Night before last, the New England people here set fire to a quantity of hay that was to have been purchased for the use of the troops at Boston, which obliges us to be more vigilant than formerly. I am glad that the money you received came so opportunely; whenever a remittance is made you shall not be forgot. My greatest desire is, to get home and settle for the remainder of my days, being, as I wrote you before, heartily tired of this way of life.

Remember me in the strongest manner to Mr. and Mrs. Inverarity and family, to Mr. and Mrs. Duval, and all acquaintances; and do not forget to inform me what day of the month my brother expired on, and the disease.

I am, D[ea]r Mother,
Your affectionate Son,
Hary Fergusson.

One year later, Hary obtained a discharge from the ship *Tartar* on the 12th of February, 1776. After this time, his whereabouts become rather mysterious. Subsequent to his 1775 letter, his friends in Scotland reportedly "never heard from, or of him" again. According to a nineteenth century writer, who may have been drawing from family tradition,

It is understood, that immediately on [Hary's] retirement from the Tartar, he opened a school in Boston, in which he taught successfully the "use of the sword and small arms." His school is said to have been well attended by the Federalists of Boston. I find, too, that he addressed a series of letters on the painfully celebrated 'Stamp Act,' to one of the Boston newspapers, in which, righteously enough certainly, he took part with the Americans.[13]

A diligent search into the Boston newspapers of the period has not, unfortunately, turned up any evidence to verify the above story. If Hary Fergusson did indeed teach fencing in Boston, he was in good company, for a number of Scots, or their students, professed to teach the "Highland style" of the back-sword, as well as the small-sword, in the city during the same period.[14]

On the title page of his published *Dictionary,* Fergusson—evincing the lyrical inclinations of his family—quotes two lines of poetry:

Ah me! what perils do environ,
the man who meddles with cold iron.

These words were extracted from *Hudibras,* a mock-heroic poem written by Samuel Butler and published during the late seventeenth century. Its epic story, echoing that of Don Quixote, contains the tale of Sir Hudibras, a knight errant who engages in numerous sword combats and feats of derring-do, in which he is frequently and absurdly defeated. Many of the poem's episodes are illustrative of how *not* to fence—such as when the protagonist is vanquished

---

13 Grossop, ci-cx.

14 This included Donald McAlpine, a "Scotch Highlander" who came to Boston in 1769 from Nova Scotia to teach art of the back-sword "in the true Highland stile"; McAlpine's protégé Robert Hewes, a member of the Sons of Liberty, who continued to teach McAlpine's method (as well as his own) for nearly fifty years in Boston; Robert Kendall, who taught the "much admired art of the Back Sword" on State Street; and J. Keith, who taught both the small-sword and the "use of the BROAD SWORD according to...the present practice in the Highlands of Scotland" at the Free-Mason's Arms in Cambridge. *Boston Evening-Post,* Dec. 11, 1769; *New England Chronicle,* Nov. 30, 1775; *Independent Chronicle,* Dec. 23, 1793; *Columbian Centinel,* July 18, 1798.

by a peasant woman because he parries too wildly—with huge, swinging motions—while his female adversary darts in "with quick and cunning slight" and "with home-made thrust...[lays] him flat upon his side." The poem serves as a fitting prelude to Fergusson's introduction, which contains an admonition to those who believe they can learn fencing by mere theory without practice. Interestingly, *Hudibras*—now all but forgotten today—is also referenced in another fencing treatise of the same period, the Irish-authored *A Few Mathematical and Critical Remarks on the Sword* (Dublin: Dr. Chamberlaine, 1781).[15]

The two lines of poetry quoted by Hary Fergusson on the title page of his *Dictionary* were, it seems, sadly prophetic for the Scottish fencing instructor. On February 2, 1779, while serving as a mariner aboard His Majesty's ship, the *Exeter*, "considering the perils and dangers of the sea and other uncertainties of this transitory life," he made out his last will and testament. Records in the National Archives of the United Kingdom show that this will was proved and executed in London on November 25, 1783 by Fergusson's "trusty friend," Mr. William Gibson of Gosport.[16] Hary Fergusson had passed into the next world.

---

15 Ben Miller, *Irish Swordsmanship: Fencing and Dueling in Eighteenth Century Ireland* (New York: Hudson Society Press, 2017), 385.

16 The National Archives; Kew, England; Prerogative Court of Canterbury and Related Probate Jurisdictions: Will Registers; Class: PROB 11; Piece: 1110.

A

DICTIONARY,

EXPLAINING THE

TERMS, GUARDS, AND POSITIONS,

USED IN THE ART OF

THE SMALL SWORD

BY

HARY FERGUSSON

Ah me! What perils do environ
The man who meddles with cold iron

HUDIBRAS

Printed in the Year MDCCLXVII

ADVERTISEMENT.

GENTLEMEN,

I f you expect a learned preface, or fulsome dedication, you will be greatly disappointed: All I intend at present, is a short compend, explaining the technical terms used in the art of fencing. —I think I need make no apology for publishing this little piece; I did it at your request, and for your advantage. In so doing, I not only obey you, but follow the example of the greatest men; and, I hope, it will be of some service to you, in learning the principles of that NOBLE SCIENCE,—the SCIENCE of DEFENCE, which nature so strongly recommends to all her children.

WHY should I tire your patience, by dwelling upon the many advantages of this branch of education? These are too obvious to be disputed.—As to the disadvantages, they are few, and necessarily attend every art of science whatever, even the most useful, the most agreeable: They are not, however, so much the natural offspring of the arts and sciences themselves, as the fatal effects of *ignorance* and *folly*.

BUT it is certainly no solid objection to learning, that a few fools make a bad use of it; no, or else the philosopher and the divine, the lawyer and physician, might bid an eternal farewell to all encouragement, to all improvement, as well as the Author.—In fine, the noble efforts of human *wit* and *ingenuity* are all too imperfect, not to be liable to the objections of the ignorant, the disingenuous, and ill-natured part of mankind, who always love to cavil, to find fault.

"Cavil they may, but never criticise."

ADIEU, then, Gentlemen! And be assured, that FENCING cannot be learned by theory; it may assist you in understanding the terms of the art, but it is PRACTICE alone that can make you ARTISTS.

I am always, Gentlemen, at the hours of teaching,

Your most obedient,

and very humble servant,

HARY FERGUSON.

POSTSCRIPT.

I AM sorry, Gentlemen, in this place, to say any thing of Mr. Locke; but your demands oblige me to mention him.—How shall I combat the greatest of men, but by opposing to him the greatest of mankind: It is well known Locke was no fencer; it is as well known that Milton was one: The former condemns an art, because he was ignorant of its principles; the latter recommends it, because he understood them.—Which of their judgments shall we believe in this important trifle? Let candour determine, and the philosopher, for once, must yield to the poet and politician.

To give satisfaction, however, to unbelieving people, I shall give them a view of Mr. Locke's objection:—"When a man is in the field, (says he) a moderate skill in fencing rather exposes him to the sword of his enemy, than secures him from it; and certainly a man of courage, who cannot fence at all, and therefore will put all on one thrust, and not stand parrying, has the odds against him who is a moderate fencer." Such is the argument of our sagacious Logician, which hardly deserves a serious refutation.—He tells his reader of a "moderate fencer," that is a fellow not master of his art, a foolish bungler, a mere blockhead. But what is that to the purpose? Is not the same objection applicable to a half-learned idiot, in any art or science whatever? Certainly such a one would still more expose himself if he engaged with an adept, since the superior knowledge of the one, endangers the ignorant folly of the other.—So far, then, is the reasoning of Mr. Locke from being an objection to the art of fencing, that it is a strong argument in its favour. Let us only oppose common sense to our ingenious metaphysician, and his quibble immediately falls to the ground.

Is not an artist supposed to be on an equal footing with his antagonist, in point of natural advantages; and has he not also all the assistance he can derive from his art! Surely, Gentlemen, you understand my meaning, or, if you do not, I shall think my labour badly bestowed.—All that I desire of you is to be above a mediocrity: A moderate fencer is still worse than a moderate poet.

A

DICTIONARY,

TO ADVANCE, to step a little forward with the right foot when your adversary is out of distance, making the left immediately follow, without altering the position of the body and legs.

TO ALLONGE, to move quickly forward the advanced arm and leg; the former fully extended, and raised as much as possible; and the latter, in a perpendicular situation betwixt the knee and ankle, (in the same instant) extending the left leg and arm, the palm of the hand being about a foot higher than the thigh, and the left foot immoveable. Tho', indeed, long stretches make a good appearance, and are greatly recommended by a number of teachers, yet, in my opinion, they are very dangerous; for, by allonging too far, you not only run the risk of falling, but are exposed to your adversary's rispost, before you have time to recover for your defence: To avoid which, keep your body up-right, and let your allonges be performed as quickly as possible, without exceeding the length of three and a half of your own feet from heel to heel.

APPEL, is a beat with your right foot, by raising it perpendicularly about two or three inches from the ground, in order to surprise your adversary.

TO ASSAULT, when swordsmen make trial of their skill either with foils of swords, they are then said to assault.

To defend yourself with the greater certainty when assaulting, observe the motion of your adversary's sword hand, and look sometime at his face to see in what temper he is; but never attempt to draw any observation from his eyes, as nothing is more dangerous and apt to mislead, especially if he squints; and whether or not, he may deceive you, by looking at one place, when he intends to deliver his thrust in another.—Observations on his sword's blade are as uncertain and fallacious, with regard to his intentions, as these on his eyes: 1st, By reason of his clearness, which often dazzles the fight.—2dly, Because of its motion being swifter than that of the hand; for as the hand is the centre, the sword's point the circumference, and the bade as it were a line drawn from the centre to the circumference, it will follow, that the parts of the sword, from the hand to the point, are more difficult to observe than the hand, as they are nearer it than the point or circumference, and therefore moved more swiftly.

ATTACK, an attempt to surprise an adversary by plain thrusts, feints, appels, &c.

ATTITUDE, the posture or position in fencing.

The most firm, easy, and graceful one, is as follows: Supposing the directions, under word Quarte; observed for the sword and sword-arm: Place the two feet at the distance of about two lengths of one of them asunder, the point of your right foot toward your adversary, and the other in such a situation, as that the lines of their direction continued, would form an angle at the left heel considerably larger than a right angle: The right knee perpendicular to the buckle of that foot, and the left so far bent, as to be perpendicular to the point of the left one; raise the left arm in a semicircular form, with the hand about the height of the head, and in the line of the shoulders, having its palm also toward your adversary: Let the head and body be erect, wearing a bold look, with a graceful and unaffected carriage.—In this position, the trunk of the body will be in a firm situation upon the legs, and but little exposed as to its breadth or length.

TO BATTER, to beat with the foible of your blade on that of your adversary, when you are going to make an attack.

TO BEAT, to put your antagonist's sword off the line, in order to procure an open, by moving only your wrist, and giving a smart jerk or dry blow with the fort of your blade on his foible.

TO BIND, to secure and cross your adversary's sword with your edge, by a pressure and spring from the wrist.—The contrary to this and the two preceding terms is disengaging: To prevent which, in the time your adversary evites[*] your binding, search for and oppose his blade on the opposite side, and if you have a sufficient open after feeling him, thrust immediately home.

BLADE, that part of a weapon which serves for defending blows or thrusts, or for attacking.—Blades are either flat or hollow, and of different lengths. Swordsmen generally wear such as are proportioned to their stature, as no real advantage can be reapt by using one of an uncommon length, as some imagine.—There are two things absolutely necessary to be taken notice of, let your blade be of what length or fashion you please; the first is, that it be

---

* *evite:* an archaic British word for avoid.

not too heavy for the mounting, which is known by laying it across your fore-finger, within about two or three inches of the hilt; and if the hilt, in that situation, counter-balances the rest of the blade, then it is well mounted; but if, on the contrary, the blade should counter-balance the mounting, then it would be too weighty before the hand, and retard a quick disengagement and parade. —The second is, That it be well tempered, which is known by fixing its point in a door or wall, and forcing it; and if the temper is good, it will bend from the point to within a foot or so of the hilt, and spring back to the former position of itself.—When blades bend and spring in this manner, they are of sufficient strength at the fort for defending, and if they do not, they are either too weak, or of a very soft temper.

BREAST-PLATE, see PLASTRON.

TO CONTRE-TEMS, to thrust at the very instant another is thrusting. A late author[*] on the sword says, "That no people are more guilty of Contre-tems than the French, by reason (as he imagines) of their imperfect Quarte and Tierce parades, and their too frequently attempting to take upon time, whereby in duels or rencounters, both parties are for the most part either killed or wounded." But this may be owing to their brisk lively temper, which makes them attack furiously without proper attention to their own defence, and not to the insufficiency of their Quarte and Tierce parades, or their endeavouring to take upon time. If, when assaulting, your adversary keeps his sword properly in line, you must take care always to secure or cross it before the delivery of your thrusts, if you would chuse to avoid Contre-tems.

---

[*]   Sir William Hope

COUNTER-PARADES, or Counter-disengagements, are defences performed with a circular motion of the sword, when an adversary evites any guard by a simple disengagement.—There are two of them, viz. in Quarte and Tierce.

THE COUNTER-PARADE in Quarte defends the feints and thrusts above the sword-arm, and is formed in the time your adversary thrusts, by dropping the point without the sword, keeping quite close to his blade, and bringing him in Quarte, by turning the edge of your fort on his foible with a firm dry beat.

THE COUNTER-PARADE in Tierce defends the thrusts and feints in Quarte, Low Quarte, and Seconde, and is formed in the time your antagonist is thrusting, by dropping the point within the sword, extending the sword arm, and bringing his sword without yours, by raising the point, with a circular motion of the wrist, in the Tierce position.—As the half-circle, the former parade, and this, not only supple the wrist, but are the best defences the art furnishes for rencounters in the dark; for a number of pokes, feints, or wide and irregular attacks, I would advise learners to practice them often, and endeavour thereby to acquire an ease and readiness in the use of them, when assaulted.

CROISE, a short foil used for parrying at the wall, and giving lessons.

DEFENCE, the art of the sword, also the cross you make upon any weapon when assaulted by an adversary.

TO DISARM, to secure your enemy's sword by the handle, when he is either thrusting, has his point off the line, or when he neglects to rispost:—To beat the sword out of one's hand with a parry.—There are more methods of disarming, than defences, in the small sword; those in Quarte and Tierce, and with the Counter-parades, are the most secure.

TO DISENGAGE, to move only the wrist and point under the hilt, from within to without the sword, or back again, without pulling them back in the time of the movement.

DISTANCE, the space that is betwixt two persons when fencing. Of distance there are three kinds:—The *first* is, When you are so near your adversary as to reach him without allonging, by only extending your sword-arm, and inclining forward the body: None who value personal safety, will fence in this distance.—The *second*, is, when you are obliged to make a full allonge before you can reach your adversary.—And the *third*, when you are obliged to advance a step or two before you can hit him with your thrust. Of these three kinds of distance, the first and third are the most dangerous.———As this article is one of the nicest in the whole art of the sword, it ought to be the object of the particular attention of every swordsman; for tho' your parade be firm, and your thrust subtle and quick, yet, if you are not thoroughly acquainted with, and practiced in the judging of distance, you may often unexpectedly be surprised with your adversary's thrust, touching you when you imagined yourself out of his reach; to prevent which, observe not to let your adversary advance toward you, without retiring as far from him, or securing his sword, and thrusting in the time he moved; but if he is one who retires much, you are to advance every time he goes back, and to gain on him the ground he lost, taking care not to be hit in the time.—If masters are careful, they will not content themselves with making their scholars practice the judging of distance when giving them lessons, but accustom them to it when they begin to assault, as then commonly their eagerness to hit, prompts them to rush furiously on their adversaries, without proper attention to distance.

TO ECART, to put any part of the body off the streight line, when you are either thrusting, feinting, or defending.

TO ENCLOSE, to come too near one's antagonist, by securing his blade, or otherwise. The being enclosed, hinders one from making a rispost any other way than by poking, and often puts it in the power of the enclose to disarm.

TO EXCHANGE THRUSTS, is to receive one from your adversary, and to return another on him before he fully recovered.

FEINT, a feint is giving your adversary to imagine you design to attack him at one part of his body, when your real intention is to thrust at some other. Feints are generally made under the blade at the small sword, and with the advance foot immoveable; there are different kinds of them, as within, without, above and below the sword, and on the same side it was presented. The best defences against Feints are the half circle and counter-parades.

FENCING, is either simple or compound. Simple fencing includes all plain thrusts and defences; and compound fencing, feints, half thrust, appells, &c.

FLANCONADE, a thrust made by engaging your antagonist's blade in Quarte, overlapping it with yours, having the thumb in Quarte position, and sending the thrust home to his flank, from which it derives its name. Flanconade is parried with Quinte, or by yielding the point of your sword to your adversary, bearing on his blade with your fort, and turning the hand and edge as in the parade, from the Quarte guard.

FOIBLE, the weak part of a sword's blade, which begins at the middle, and ends at the point.

FOIL, a blunt sword (having a button at the end of the blade) generally about 38 or 40 inches in length inclusive of the mounting, used for learners to practise with.—To buy foil blades, observe the directions under the word BLADE.

FORT, that Part which begins at the shell or guard, and ends at the middle of the sword's blade; it is properest for parrying, and strictly speaking, every thrust should be defended with it.

A person's foible may become his fort, or his fort his foible, according to the binding and pressure of his blade on that of his adversary, or by the pressure of his adversary's blade on his; for example, if with nine inches from the point of my sword, which is a part of my foible, I secure five or six inches of my adversary's, yet the part of the blade with which I bound and overpowered his, may be called the fort, because it had the same effect as if it had been really that part.—Again, should my fort, a foot from the hilt, be overpowered with only seven or eight inches of my adversary's blade, it would be of no more service against him than the Foible, from the command his sword had over it.

GRIPE, or GRASPE, that part of the sword's hilt, which you hold in your hand, it ought to be proportioned to the length of your fingers, and breadth of your hand.

GUARD, the posture one puts himself into for his greater security when fencing. There are only five guards belonging to the small sword, *viz.* the PRIME, SECONDE, TIERCE, QUARTE, and QUINTE, which last is by some called OCTAVE.—Tho' these guards contribute much to secure one, it is only the parade made from them which can justly be called a defence, as people may keep very close guards, and form but wide and uncertain defences from them: The half-circle and the counters in Quarte and Tierce are not guards, but parades, as they are formed from some of the above five.

HALF CIRCLE, a parade, by making with the wrist and point a semicircle from right to left, raising and extending the arm, with the nails of the fingers well up. The half-circle is not only a good defence for feints, but for most thrusts of the sword.

HALF SWORD, is being within distance, so that one can easily engage the foible of his adversary's blade with his fort.

TO HALF THRUST, to advance your point in the line you presented it, as if to thrust, and to beat with the sole of your right foot on the floor, or ground, without advancing it, in order to make your adversary lose his position, and procure you an open.

HANDLE, see GRIPE.

* HANGING GUARD, the method of forming this guard, is by turning the nail of the thumb quite downward, with the hand higher than the head, raising and extending the arm, the right shoulder close to the right ear, the point of the sword well sloped,

and inclining a little to the left. If cuts are thrown for either the inside of your body, arm or face, when thus in guard, turn your wrist and edge to the left for your defence, and if thrown for any part of the contrary side, to the right.—This is the safest guard of the broad or back sword, as it secures, in a manner, every part, except the advanced leg, which you ought to slip back when it is attacked, and in the time, cut your adversary's sword arm, with your hand exactly in the Seconde position.

HILT, the head or mounting of a sword composed of four parts, the Gripe, Pommel, Shell or Guard, and Back-Ward.

* INSIDE GUARD, is made by holding the sword arm and blade as high as in the Quarte position, turning the nails of the fingers a little more downward.—From this guard, are formed defences for all cuts made at the inside of the belly, face, or sword arm.

LOW QUARTE, or QUARTE COUPEE, a thrust, by disengaging subtilely from Quarte, sloping the point under your adversary's guard, extending and raising the arm, having the hand in the Quarte position, and the right foot a few inches off the line to the left side; when the thrust is finished, recover with a firm beat in Tierce.—Another and better way of thrusting low Quarte: When engaged without the sword, either in Tierce or Quarte over the arm, disengage the point under the hilt, thrust full home with the hand in the Quarte position, and recover as above.——LOW QUARTE is parry'd with the Half-Circle, Quinte, or Seconde.

MARK, a wafer, or any piece of paper or leather of its size affixed to the wall of the school, by practicing at which, scholars are taught to thrust quickly, and plant well.

MEASURE, (to break) when you are certain your adversary's thrust, without advancing, will only over-reach the nearest parts of your body, a few inches; bend it quickly back, supporting your weight by the left leg, and keeping the right foot immoveable.— Should your antagonist advance and re-double his thrust, or offer to take you on the time of recovering your body to its former position, you are then to retire, parry and rispost.

* MEDIUM GUARD, the arm wrist and sword in this guard, ought to be kept in the same height as the Quarte, and the edge of the sword perpendicular to the ground. This position is of more use in the offensive, than the defensive part of the sword.

TO MISPLANT, not to direct any thrust properly.

MOUNTING, the HILT of a sword, see HILT.

OPEN, any part of your antagonist, or yourself that is not guarded: Opens are procured by Feints, Beats, Appells, and by Binding the Sword.

* OUTSIDE GUARD, is formed exactly like the Tierce, except that you must keep the arm a little more pliable. This guard defends any cut made at the outside of the body or arm.

TO PALM, to put off or defend any thrust with the palm of the hand, by turning the points of the fingers downward, and the back of the hand to the right.

PARADE, the defence or dry beat you make from any guard, when your adversary is thrusting. A parade ought to be done with the fort of the blade on the foible, so timed, as to meet and put off your antagonist's thrust in the twinkling of an eye, altho' delivered pretty near, and of such strength and smartness, as to hinder him from forcing your sword to effectuate his design in thrusting.

TO PARRY, to defend or put aside a thrust. A parry differs from the preceeding term in this that it can be done when one stands to no regular guard.

A PASS; as passes are safer in fencing-schools with foils, than with sword in hand in the field, I shall give no larger description of them, than that they are thrusts preceeded by an allonge, with the left foot more advanced than the right; and shall earnestly advise such as are teachers, to substitute some more useful lessons in their place.

TO PLANT, to direct any thrust when fencing. The surest way to become dexterous at planting, is to thrust often Quarte and Tierce at the wall.

PLASTRON, or B R E A S T - P L A T E, a piece of stuffed leather, which masters use when they teach their scholars, in order to prevent hurts in their breasts.

POKE, a thrust made by pulling back the sword arm, either without or with a disengagement.

POMMEL, a little ball at the end of the Hilt, sometimes a round, and sometimes of an oval shape, used to keep the parts of the hilt firm, and to make a sword light at the point.

POSITION, POSTURE, two words used in describing the different situations of the body, sword, arm, legs, &c. See ATTI-TUDE.

PREVOT, an usher or under teacher in an academy or fenc-ing-school.

PRIME, a guard, formed by turning the wrist to the left, the nail of the thumb downward, the nails of the fingers toward the right, looking over your elbow to your adversary; it is the most proper guard to form a parade from, for all the thrusts forced in Tierce or Quarte over the arm. The thrust is delivered within the hand, in the above position.

QUARTE, this guard is formed by holding the wrist about the height of the pit of the stomach, keeping the right arm flexible, having the thumb quite upward on the flat side of the handle, the fore finger a little nearer the guard of the sword than the thumb, the back of the hand to the right, the nails of the fingers inclining upward, and toward the left, the point of the sword two or three inches more elevated than the mounting, the elbow kept well to the left, and the shoulder, thumb, and point on the same direction. Quarte is the strongest position of any, the best for offending, and when formed agreeable to the above directions, will, by the least movement, secure one from all thrusts within, without, below, and above the sword; which could not be done but by a very great one, if kept as some persons form it, with the joint of the wrist as much as possible to the left, and the thumb and sword's blade inclining to the right; such a position will not only give great opens without, above, and below the sword, but the wide turn that must be made to defend the thrusts directed to these parts, is more tiresome and straining for the arm than the former Quarte position, not to mention the time lost by it. For the position of the body, head, arms, &c. See ATTITUDE.

QUARTE, is thrust within the sword, by raising the wrist as high as the forehead, extending the arm, and allonging in the above position. It is parried without putting the arm off the line, by turning the hand and edge a little to the inside.

QUARTE COUPEE, see LOW QUARTE.

QUARTE OVER THE ARM, is thrust without the sword, with the hand in the Quarte position, and parry'd with Tierce, the half circle, or by beating the sword to the right, with the thumb in the Quarte position.

QUINTE, the sword hand when forming this guard, is in the same position as the Quarte, you only slope the point, extend the arm, and carry your wrist a little to the right. This posture is more constrained than any of the other four; Quinte parry's Seconde, Low Quarte, Quarte and Flanconade, and is thrust with the hand in the above position.

TO RECOVER, is, after an allonge, to bring the body to the same position it was in before the delivery of any thrust, by bending back the left knee, and reposing your whole weight upon it, taking back the right leg, free from the surface of the floor or ground, and replacing it in its former position.

TO REDOUBLE, is when you are within distance, to make the same thrust again, if you misplanted it the first time, and have a proper open. Redoubling is very dangerous, especially, if your adversary depends on the quickness of his risposte, and makes of the use of that kind of play.

TO RETIRE, to step back with the left foot, when your adversary is too near, making the right follow, without altering the distance that was between the heels before retiring.

TO RISPOSTE, to give a quick and smart return of a thrust for your adversary's body, after having defended the one he made at you.

ROUND PARADES, see C O U N T E R P A R A D E S.

* ST. GEORGE'S GUARD, is a cross one, used for defending the head and face, and is formed by moving the advanced leg about a foot to the right, bending well the knees, keeping the belly back, the hilt higher than the head, crossing the face with the blade, the hand in the Seconde position, and the point well sloped.

SALUTE, by this word in fencing schools, is meant beats with the advanced foot, and flourishes with the sword. When a young person goes to school, the salute is the first thing to be learned, tho' of no more service in fencing, than dashing and flourishing in the art of writing; as you may see by the following description, which I give more for the satisfaction of such as are curious, than for any other purpose. The Salute has five different positions.

FIRST POSITION, engage your adversary's blade at the foible in Tierce, make two beats with the heel; and one with the sole of your shoe, extend both legs and thighs, raise your hand with ease, and take off your hat without moving the head.

SECOND POSITION, being the right foot behind the left, and let the point of the shoe be about two inches farther back than the left heel, at the same time, extend the right arm, with the hand as high as the head in the Quarte position, and as much as possible toward the right, the point of the sword lower than the mounting, the left arm extend, the hat kept firm in the hand and its crown outward, about two feet higher than the thigh.

THIRD POSITION, turn the wrist to the left, keep the arm pliable at the elbow, and the point of the sword to your adversary's right shoulder, the other parts of your body in the former position.

FOURTH POSITION, after saluting to the left, turn the hand in tierce, keep the arm, and the point of your sword opposite to your adversary's body, and then place yourself in guard, by bringing the left foot back the distance of two shoe-lengths from the right; in the same instant put on your hat, and round the left arm in the form of a half-circle.

FIFTH POSITION, after turning the hand in Tierce, make the same beats you did formerly, extend the legs and thighs, bring the left foot about three inches before the point of the right; instantly extend both arms, turn the hand in Quarte, the left arm about two feet distant from the left high, the right hand as high as the eye, with the point of the blade a little sloped, and toward your adversary.—When this is finished, place yourself in the Quarte guard.

SANDAL, a light pump wanting the heel, made fast on the foot, with leather thongs, used when fencing.

SECONDE, in forming his guard, the elbow and wrist ought to be raised almost as high as the shoulder, the nail of the thumb downward, the nails of the fingers toward the right, and the back of the hand to the inside or left.

SECONDE, is generally thrust from Tierce, with the hand in the above position, by turning the point a little to the left, and raising the wrist and arm higher than the head. It is parried with Quarte, Quinte, the Circle, or the Seconde guard.

SWORD, a weapon used either for offending or defending. —Its parts are the blade and mounting; the former preserved by the scabbard, to which belong the hook and chape. To hold the sword, see QUARTE.

TIERCE, is either formed from Seconde, by sinking the arm at the elbow and wrist, and raising the point a little higher than mounting; or from Quarte, by turning the edge of the blade outward, the back of the hand quite upward, with the nail of the fingers quite down. The sword hand, in forming Tierce, makes a full quarter of a circle from Quarte, and is a more constrained posture. It is thrust above and without the sword, with the nail of the thumb downward; and parried, by extending the arm, and turning the edge to the right.

TO THRUST, to hit your adversary with the point of your sword. The thrust under the hilt, such as Low Quarte, Quarte, and Seconde, are performed with more ease than those in Quarte over the arm, and Tierce, by reason of the natural tendency people's hands have to fall low in disengaging. Every thrust ought to be delivered close to the blade, and as near to the guard of the sword as possible; and in order to thrust quickly, never offer to disengage, until your sword's point be advanced beyond your antagonist's hilt, upon the same side it was presented. —If you observe this, and extend the left leg, making the upper part of the body project farther than the belly, with the sword hand in motion before the advanced foot, you can never fail in making a quick thrust.

THESE farther observations may be useful as to thrusting.

1st, SUCH thrusts as are directed to the breast and ribs often have not a proper effect, as these are the strongest parts of the body, and most difficult to penetrate.

2dly, THRUSTS, when directed to any part, are the shorter and weaker, the more the hand is turned to Quarte, or the left from the constrained posture of the arm.

3dly, A number of masters make their scholars ecart and couch their heads the contrary way they thrust, in order, as they say, to prevent hurts in the face, whereas nothing is more absurd; for, in my opinion, this ecarting and couching rather exposes than secures them from danger; for, if your adversary defends you in Quarte, when your head is couched to the right, and risposts in Quarte over the arm, or tierce, he would certainly hit you in the face, as the head, by ecarting, is so much inclined forward, as to make you lose the balance of your body, and consequently be slow in recovering.

TIME, by thrusting on Time in fencing, is meant hitting your adversary, when he is going to thrust or advance, without in the least offering to parry, cross, or oppose his sword.

The following are the most convenient ways of thrusting on Time.

1st, WHEN your adversary is raising his right foot to advance.

2dly, WHEN he is making any feint, not preceded by a binding or securing your blade.

3dly, WHEN he is making half thrusts under the blade, by pushing full home at the same time above, or when he half thrusts above, by pushing under.

4thly, By thrusting, while he is avoiding your blade by disengaging.

TO TRAVERSE, in fencing, signifies to go off the line in a circular manner, either for safety, procuring opens, or to hinder the sun-beams from dazzling the eye-sight, if assaulting in the field.

TO VOLT, is when your adversary thrusts, to bring the left foot toward the right side as far as you can, without advancing it; to oppose, the left hand, and to thrust at the same time with the arm fully extended, and the wrist as high as the head in the Quarte position. There are other kinds of Volts, but all dangerous; and altho' they may sometimes succeed, yet the thrusts delivered from them are so weak, as scarcely to penetrate any part of the body.

WALL, (to thrust at) when two persons thrust and parry Quarte and Tierce alternately: The point of the defender's left foot is always to be placed to the wall of the room or school, that he may not avoid his antagonist's thrusts, by breaking measure, or retiring.

WARD, that part of the hilt in form, of a half circle, which comes from the shell, and is fixed in the pommel.—Its use is to preserve the fingers in fencing.

WITHIN THE SWORD, WITHOUT THE SWORD, The first term is the distance between the sword-arm and left side, and the second, that on the opposite one.

FINIS.

SHOLTO DOUGLAS SORLIE

I n 1788, a decision was made to standardize cavalry swords in
Great Britain. A directive issued in January of that year stipu-
lated that it was "his Majesty's intention to have an inspection of
all the regimental swords in order to fix upon one for general use."
This resulted in an order for a new sword to be designed and
produced, which both officers and their soldiers would conform
to. More than eight years later, on November 14, 1796, a royal
warrant authorized a new pattern of light cavalry sword, and gave
details for a new heavy cavalry sword as well.[17] In tandem with the
issuance of the new sword design, an effort was also made to
reform and standardize the method of sword exercise used by the
British cavalry. As a result, several treatises on the sword exercise
for cavalry were published in 1796 and in the years immediate
following.

---

17 John Wilkinson Latham, *British Military Swords* (New York: Crown
Publishers, Inc., 1966), 29-33.

The new sword exercise was the brainchild of Major-General John Gaspard Le Marchant (1766–1812), a British career soldier from the isle of Guernsey. According to Le Marchant's memoirs, his own training in the use cavalry sword began only a few years prior to the publication of his influential treatise, around 1793 or 1794:

The idea of it was originally suggested to his mind during his campaigns in Flanders, by the many instances of discomfiture which our dragoons experienced in single combat with the enemy. Full of the importance of providing a remedy for so serious an evil, he put himself under the tuition of a serjeant in the Austrian cavalry, from whom he learned the little that was then practised in that service; and not finding his views much forwarded by this assistance, he sought every opportunity of consulting with all individuals among the different armies, who were distinguished for their practical skill in the use of the sword. The immense body of cavalry in the field, and the diversity of the nations of which it was composed, materially aided his researches. No sooner, however, did he set about the formation of a Code of Instruction from what he had thus gathered abroad, than he saw how impossible it was to reconcile such unconnected materials, and he was obliged to begin by creating a system of exercise, combining attack and defence, upon principles almost entirely his own...he accordingly submitted to the consideration of the Duke of York, the Code of Instruction under which he proposed to train the whole British Cavalry in the use of the sword; and after due personal inquiry from His Royal Highness, and the report of a Committee of General Officers in its favour, the proposed code received unqualified approbation, and was established under Royal authority among the permanent regulations of the Cavalry. Orders were then issued to Major Le Marchant to begin his course of instruction with all possible dispatch, and on his suggestion detachments from every regiment of Regular and Fencible Cavalry in Great Britain, consisting of an officer and twenty men, were assembled at different periods, at four

From the first (1796) edition of Le Marchant's *Exercise*.

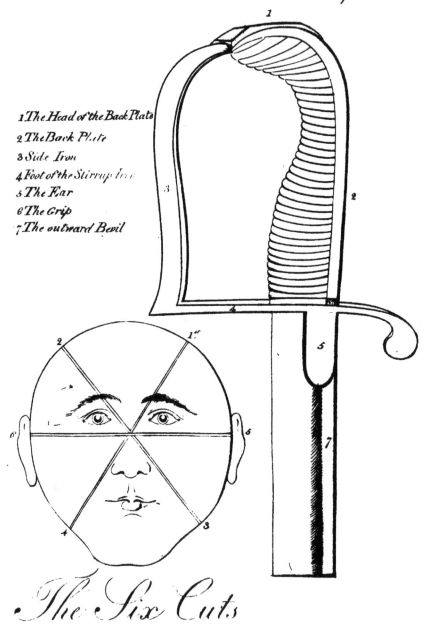

A Blade Mounted with a Stirrup Hilt.

1 The Head of the Back Plate
2 The Back Plate
3 Side Iron
4 Foot of the Stirrup Iron
5 The Ear
6 The Grip
7 The outward Bevil

The Six Cuts

From the 1797 edition of Le Marchant's *Exercise*.

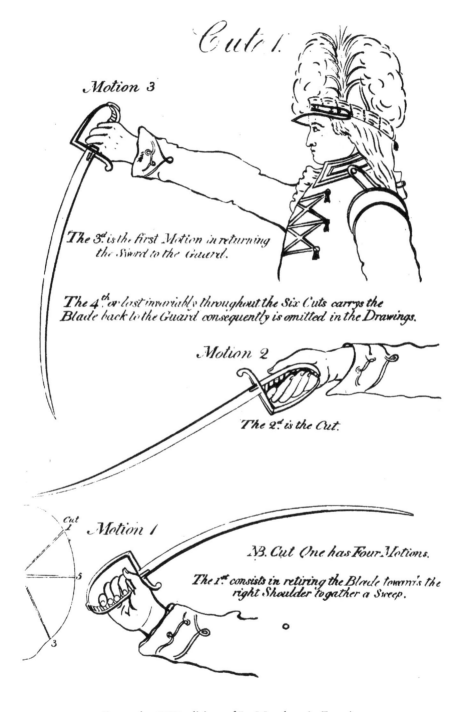

From the 1797 edition of Le Marchant's *Exercise*.

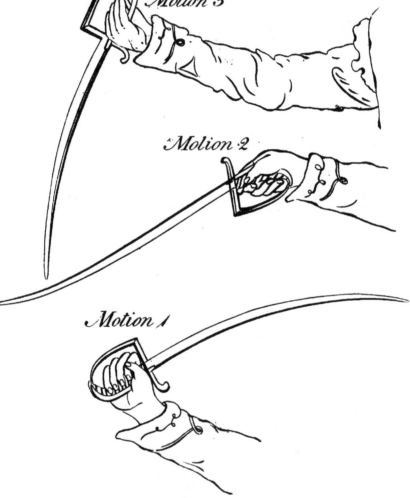

Cut 2

Motion 3

Motion 2

Motion 1

Motion one consists in returning the Blade
towards the left Shoulder.
Two is the Cut.
Three the first Motion in returning to the Guard.
Four is the Guard.

From the 1797 edition of Le Marchant's *Exercise*.

distinct stations, where, in the course of six months, he completed their instruction in the practices and evolutions of the new exercise...[18]

Le Marchant's treatise on his new method, the *Rules and Regulations for the Sword Exercise of the Cavalry,* was first published in 1796, selling "many thousands of copies," and would be widely reprinted throughout Britain, Ireland, and the United States.[19] That the exercise met with great enthusiasm is evinced by the fact that the next several years saw the publication of numerous additional treatises on Le Marchant's method. This included two books issued to the Yeomanry, which had also received instruction in the new exercise.[20] In 1797, W. Pepper, of the of the Nott's Yeomanry Cavalry, published his *Abridgment of the new broad sword exercise*[21], and Richard Lawrence released a series of colorful plates, entitled *To the officers and privates of the four troops of Warwickshire Yeomenry Cavalry* "representing the eight principal motions in the attack and defence."[22] Additionally, the same year, Richard Leach, a sergeant in the Norfolk Rangers, published his *Words of command, and a brief explanation embellished with engravings, representing the various cuts and attitudes of the new sword exercise.*[23] And

18 Denis Le Marchant, *Memoirs of the late Major General Le Marchant* (London: Samuel Bentley, 1841), 44-47.

19 Ibid., 48. Hewes's American editions of the exercise were published in Boston and Philadelphia in 1802, in Baltimore in 1812, and in Middlebury, Vermont in 1814.

20 Le Marchant, 47.

21 W. Pepper, *An Abridgment of the New Broad Sword Exercise: By W. Pepper, of the Nott's Yeomanry Cavalry* (London: Printed for the author, 1797)

22 Richard Lawrence, *To The Officers and Privates of the four troops of Warwickshire Yeomenry Cavalry, These plates representing the eight principal motions in the attack and defence as practised in the Hungarian Sword Exercise' Richard Lawrence of the 2nd Troop* ([Birmingham: 1797]).

23 Richard Leach, *Words of command, and a brief explanation embellished with engravings, representing the various cuts and attitudes of the new sword exercise*

Left Parry.

J. Wigley. Sc

Published according to Act March 15.th 1797 & sold by W. Pepper: Nottingham.

From W. Pepper's 1797 *Abridgment* of Le Marchant's exercise.

(Newcastle: 1797).

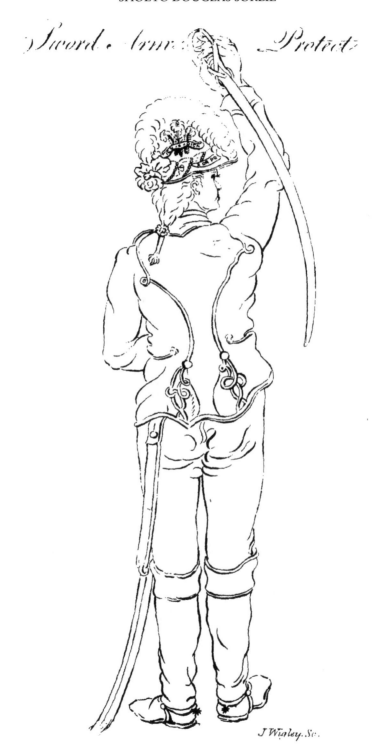

Sword. Arm~ ... Protect

From W. Pepper's 1797 *Abridgment* of Le Marchant's exercise.

J.Wigley.Sc.

St George.

From W. Pepper's 1797 *Abridgment* of Le Marchant's exercise.

during that winter, yet another treatise on Le Marchant's system was authored and published by a young Scot, and member of the 7th Queen's Own Regiment of Light Dragoons, named Sholto Douglas Sorlie. This treatise, until now, has evaded the attention of scholars and historians.

* * *

Few details of Sorlie's life are known beyond those found in his military records. He was later described as the veteran of many battles, and a "a good officer and a brave soldier." His obituary declares that he was born on "the 21st of December, 1771"[24], whereas a baptismal record places his birth on December 22, 1772. Whatever the actual date, we know that Sholto Douglas Sorlie was born in Edinburgh, Scotland, the son of James Sorlie and Margaret Ferguson.[25] In 1791 he enlisted as a private in the 7th Queen's Own Regiment of Light Dragoons, and quickly rose through the ranks as a non-commissioned officer—becoming a corporal and then a sergeant within the span of a few years. In December, 1796, he was appointed to the rank of sergeant major.[26]

Beginning in April of 1797, while still a member of the 7th Light Dragoons, Sorlie began publishing his own treatise on Le Marchant's new sword exercise. This text initially appeared in several installments among the pages of *The Sporting Magazine.* Later that year, a first edition in book format was released by John Debrett, a London publisher, under the title: *The Words of*

24 *Leeds Times*, November 2, 1839.

25 Ancestry.com. Scotland, select Births and Baptisms, 1564-1950. Provo, UT, UsA: Ancestry.com Operations, Inc., 2014. FHL Film Number: 1066686; Reference ID: 2:17PGDXG.

26 National Archives, Return of Services, Reference # WO 25/774/146.

Command, and a brief Explanation of the New Sword Exercise.[27] A review of this book, appearing that winter in the *Monthly Review,* stated:

> We are always pleased when we see military men *studying* their profession; and we cheerfully announce this treatise as useful to young officers. To have made it complete, however, Mr. Sorlie should have enlarged his plan, and distinctly described every motion by which the different cuts and parries are performed.[28]

Although Sorlie's text is, as is to be expected, similar to Le Marchant's original in many ways (and to the other parallel treatments of the sword exercise), it contains many differences and additions of note. Among the most distinctive is its specificity in how to target the adversary's body—something that is rather neglected in Le Marchant's text. For instance, whereas Le Marchant instructs the reader to deliver various numbered cuts to the "face", "thigh," and "body" of one's adversary, Sorlie provides greater detail in how to make those cuts:

> You will now explain to them the use of the six cuts as follows: cut one is to cut a man from his left ear to his right shoulder; cut two, from the right ear to his left shoulder: cut three and cut four, are in case a man raises his arm in cutting one or two, (that is to say is off his guard) to cut him under the wrist; and cut five and six are to cut across, cut five to the left, and cut six to the right.

There is a certain brutal immediacy to Sorlie's direct, unsanitized language—recalling the attitudes of earlier Scottish writers on the subject of swordsmanship, such as Donald McBane. He also includes unusual observations most likely gleaned from experience, such as the following:

---

27 *Monthly Magazine,* December, 1797.

28 Ibid.

The back of the sword must be turned towards the horse's crup; also in cutting three and four, that the sword is carried strait out to the front, in order to save the horse's head; for if a horse gets one cut, it makes him ever after shy.

As in Le Marchant's original, Sorlie also includes instruction in how the cavalry man may defend against members of the bayonet-wielding infantry, and defense against multiple simultaneous opponents.

Interestingly, during the autumn of 1797—only a few months following the initial publication of Sorlie's treatise—John Gaspard Le Marchant himself joined Sorlie's unit, the 7th Queen's Light Dragoons. Le Marchant had recently been promoted to the rank of lieutenant-colonel, and was now to serve as second-in-command of the 7th under Lord Paget.[29] Thus did Sholto Sorlie find himself in the perfect situation to hone his knowledge of the new sword exercise, from the very man who had devised it.

One can only wonder if Le Marchant approved of the actions of his young sergeant major, in publishing his own treatment of the exercise. The coincidence of their sudden service together is rather striking. Had they known each other prior to 1797? Had Sorlie, perhaps, somehow already benefited from Le Marchant's personal instruction? Or had he simply read a copy of the 1796 treatise, or received instruction in the sword exercise from another officer to whom it had been previously disseminated? As far as we currently know, the records do not tell. Whatever the case, Sorlie seems to have been treated favorably during his service under Le Marchant. The next year, he was given the senior position of quartermaster of the regiment[30], and would see his treatise published in a second

---

29 R. H. Thoumine, *Scientific Soldier, A Life of General Le Marchant, 1766–1812* (London: Oxford University Press, 1968), 39-60.

30 National Archives, Return of Services, Reference # WO 25/774/146.

Major-General John Gaspard Le Marchant, pictured in his *Memoirs*.

London edition by Debrett[31], as well as in an American edition by William Cobbett, a British publisher who had relocated to Philadelphia (though it is uncertain if this last edition was issued with Sorlie's approval). This Philadelphia edition was simply titled, *A treatise on the new sword exercise, for cavalry.*[32]

Sholto Sorlie would go on to have a distinguished military career. In the following decade, he served extensively in the Napoleonic conflicts, taking part in numerous battles. By February, 1806, he had left the Queen's Own Dragoons, and held the rank of Ensign in the 96th Infantry. On the 25th of April, 1806, he purchased a Lieutenancy for himself in the 46th Regiment of Foot. Later in 1806, he moved from the 46th to the 68th Regiment.[33] On July 22, 1812, Sorlie reportedly took part in the Battle of Salamanca, among the forces under the Duke of Wellington, during the course of which Major-General Le Marchant was killed.[34]

On August 31, 1815, Sorlie was moved from the 68th to the 1st Royal Veteran Batallion, "in consequence of ill health and impaired vision contracted upon service," retaining his rank of Lieutenant.[35] On January 25, 1820, he was promoted to Adjutant of the 4th Royal Veteran Battallion.[36]

Late in life, in the year 1837, Sorlie was living in Leeds on Darley street, where he owned a house.[37] The life of Sholto

31 *London Evening Mail,* May 30, 1798.

32 Sholto Sorlie, *A treatise on the new sword exercise, for cavalry* (Philadelphia: Re-published by William Cobbett, 1798).

33 *London Gazette,* December 30, 1806. National Archives, Return of Services, Reference # WO 25/774/146.

34 *Leeds Times,* November 2, 1839. See also the *Leeds Mercury* and *Leeds Intelligencer* of the same date.

35 *London Gazette,* September 9, 1815. National Archives, Return of Services, Reference # WO 25/774/146.

36 *London Morning Post,* February 3, 1820.

37 *The Poll Book of the Leeds Borough Election, July, 1837* (Leeds: R. Perring,

Douglas Sorlie came to an end two years later, when it was reported that, on the 29th of October:

> Tuesday last, at Leeds, [died] Lieut. and Adjt. Sholto Douglas Sorlie, formerly of the 68th Regiment of Light Infantry, late of the 2nd Veteran Battalion. Of his service—Lieut. Sorlie was at the Battles of Salamanca, Vittoria, Pyrenees, Navelle, Orthes, Peninsular, &c.; he was a good officer and a brave soldier. Sorlie was born on the 21st of December, 1771, therefore died his 68th year.[38]

1837), 53.

38 *Leeds Times*, November 2, 1839. See also the *Leeds Mercury* and *Leeds Intelligencer* of the same date.

NOTE TO THE READER

No copies of the first or second London editions of Sorlie's treatise are known to have survived. The fact of their existence, however, is indisputable, due to extant references in the *Monthly Magazine* of December, 1797, and to an advertisement in the *Evening Mail* of May 30, 1798. For the purposes of both clarity and layout, the text of Sorlie's treatise (presented here) has been taken from both the earlier 1797 printing, published sequentially in the *Sporting Magazine,* and Sorlie's subsequent 1798 Philadelphia edition, which are nearly identical, but which vary slightly, and contain alternately superior elements.

TREATISE

ON THE

New Sword Exercise,

FOR CAVALRY.

—

By *SHOLTO SORLIE,*

OF THE SEVENTH (OR QUEEN'S OWN) REGIMENT OF LIGHT DRAGOONS.

—

"Without discipline, Soldiers are but an armed mob."
MARSHAL SAXE.

New Sword Exercise.

The WORDS *of* COMMAND, *and a*
brief Explanation of the NEW SWORD EXERCISE. *By Sholto*
Sorlie, Serjeant in the 7th, or
Queen's own regiment of Light-
Dragoons.

TYPE OF THE SIX CUTS,
No. 2. No. 1.
No. 6. No. 5.
No. 4. No. 3.

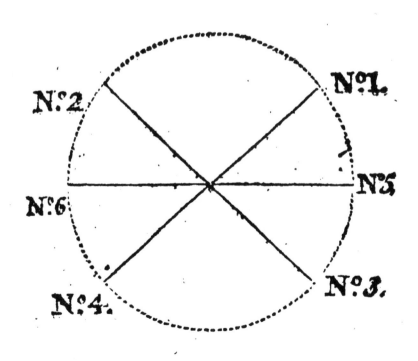

—

Words of Command for the SWORD EXERCISE.

Draw swords—prepare to perform the sword Exercise—march.

First Division.

Prepare to guard—guard—assault—left protect—right protect—prepare to guard—to the front give point—prepare to guard—guard—slope sword.

Second Division.

Prepare to guard—guard—assault—guard—bridle arm protect—sword arm protect—Saint George—to the rear cut—guard—slope sword.

Third Division.

Prepare to guard—guard—assault—guard—horse near side protect—off-side protect—cuts, 1, 2, and 1.—left protect—right protect—prepare to guard—to the front give point—cut 1.—guard—slope swords.

Fourth Division.

Prepare to guard—guard—on your right to the front party—cut 2 and 1—to the right give point—prepare to guard—to the left give point—cut 3 and 4—guard-slope swords.

Fifth Division.

Prepare to guard—guard—on your near side cut 1 and 2—off-side cut 1 and 2—left give point—prepare to guard—right give point—cut 5 and 6—guard—slope swords.

Sixth Division.

Prepare to guard—guard—to the right give point—cut 1 and 2—left parry—left protect—right protect—to the front give point—prepare to guard—slope swords.

The Words of Command when performed by Fugel Men.

Draw swords—prepare to perform the sword exercise—march.

Perform the sword exercise in six divisions of movements, by fugel men—first division—second division—third division—fourth division—fifth division—sixth division—to the front form—march.

Words of Command for the Grounds of the Sword Exercise.

Draw swords—prepare to guard—guard—assault—guard—prepare to guard—left protect—right protect—prepare to guard—guard—horse near side protect—off-side protect—prepare to guard—guard—bridle arm protect—sword arm protect—Saint George—to the rear cut—against infantry, to the right give point—right to the rear parry—cut 3.—left give point—left to the rear parry—cut 4.—against cavalry, to the front give point—cut 5 and 6—guard—slope swords.

Drill Motions Explained.

The first thing that is to be taught a beginner or a recruit, are the drill motions. They will form a rank entire; should there be more than twelve, they must be doubled, as they will take up too much ground for one person to have his eye on them all, to see that they are right. Having your drill fell in at their proper interval from each other, you will give the word,

Draw Swords,

Which is to be done at three motions, viz. 1st, Bring the right hand smart across the body, putting the hand into the sword knot, and giving it two or three turns in order to fasten it on the wrist, seize hold of the hilt of the sword, and draw it about six inches out of the scabbard. 2d. Extend the right arm well up over the head, bring the sword in an upright direction with the point upwards, and the right hand with the hilt of the sword just below the chin. 3d. Bring the sword smart down, edge of the sword to the front elbow and wrist in a line, with the back of the sword in a line with the right eye. This last position is called carry swords.—

Prepare to guard.

At this word of command, the sword and bridle hand are to be brought smart up together, the bridle hand just above the navel, and the sword hand over the bridle hand, the flat side of the sword to the front, and carried upright, with the blade touching against the peak of the men's helmets.—

Guard.

At this word of command, the bridle hand remains fast, the sword is darted strait out to the front, in such direction, that the man can just see through the clips or ears of the sword: the point of the sword laying strait across to the left, and the back of the sword turned a little up to receive a blow.

The next thing to be taught are the six cuts, or the assault, which are all to be taught by motions, that is, cut one in four motions, cut two in four motions, cut three in three, cut four in three, cut five in three, and cut six in three motions. When perfect in cut one by the drill motions, teach them to do it in one motion. When perfect in cut two by the drill motions, they must be taught to join cut one and two together, and so on until they can join the six cuts. You will now explain to them the use of the six cuts as follows: cut one is to cut a man from his left ear to his right shoulder; cut two, from the right ear to his left shoulder: cut three and cut four, are in case a man raises his arm in cutting one or two, (that is to say is off his guard) to cut him under the wrist; and cut five and six are to cut across, cut five to the left, and cut six to the right. You will next explain to them that there are five guards to the front, three for the protection of the man, and two for the horse; the use of the first guard to the front, which is that called guard, save cut one and two, and by lowering the hand a little, saves cut three and four; the second guard, which is left protect, saves cut five, and giving point to the left; the third guard, which is right protect, saves cut six, and giving point to the right; the fourth guard, which is horse near side protect, saves cut one at your horse's head; and the fifth guard, which is off-side protect, saves cut two at your horse's head.

You will next explain to them, that there are three guards to the rear; the first, which is bridle arm protect, saves the whole of the left side from a cut in the rear. This guard is first to be taught in two motions, and when perfect in it, by two motions, learn them to do it in one. The second guard to the rear, which is sword arm protect, saves the whole of the right side from a cut in the rear. The third, which is called Saint George, saves the head; from the

Saint George, you will teach them to cut to the rear in two motions; when perfect in cutting it by two motions, learn them to do it in one.

You will next teach them to give point against infantry, by the word two, and parrying to the rear, next giving point to the front against cavalry.—

Slope swords.

This position is come to, by letting the back of the sword lay upon the right shoulder, the right elbow close to the body, and the sword-hand in a line with the elbow. When you have got your men perfect in the grounds of it, so as they can go through it by fugle men[39], you will proceed to teach them the six divisions of movements by word of command, as before shewn.

---

39 "FUSIL-*man*, commonly called *fugle-man*, is a non-commissioned officer or soldier, whose duty is to give the time for the several motions of the firelock, the facings, &c. performed by any body of men. His post is usually in front, commonly towards the right flank; but common sense points out that it should always be more centrical, especially for whole regiments, the rear ranks of which are often compelled to perform their motions partly by guess, and partly by a rapid adaptation of what they see doing by the front rank. This inconvenience is necessarily increased in proportion to the obliquity or deviation from a central position. The motions of the fusil-man should, in contradistinction to those of the soldiers in general, be broad, open, and strongly marked...Without such demonstrations, which certainly appear individually ludicrous, no corps could go through their motions with exactness." Abraham Rees, *The Cyclopædia; Or, Universal Dictionary of Arts, Sciences, and Literature, Vol. XV* (London: Longman, Hurst, Rees, Orme, & Brown, 1819).

—

The Method of preparing to perform the Six Divisions of Movements on Foot.

—

The fugle-men will place themselves about fifty yards in front of the drill; one on the right flank, and the other on the left, and to take care that they out-flank the drill well, otherwise the files in the rear will not be able to see them.

Should it only be a large drill, it will be fell in rank entire, the swords hanging down by the slings, the men having hold of the scabbard between the fore-finger and thumb of the left hand, and the right hand down by the thigh, until the word of command is given,

From the right ease your files.

At which word of command, the right-hand man standing fast, the whole of the other men will bend their right arms at the elbow, resting their hands on their hips, and taking so much distance from their right-hand men, as barely to touch their left arms with their right elbows.

When got their proper distance, and steady, you will give the word,

Right hands as they were.

They will now be ordered to tell themselves off, which is done as follows: the right-hand man will turn his head to the left, and say with a distinct voice, *right.* The next to him turning his head the same way, will say, *centre,* and the next *left,* the next *right,* the next *centre,* and the next *left,* and so on, until they are told off. Having your drill told off, you will give the word,

Draw Swords.

Which is to be done as was explained in the drill motions: swords being drawn, you will give the word,

Prepare to perform the sword exercise;

At which word of command, the first centre, and left file on the right, will fall back for pivets covering the right file: the centre file taking three, and the left file six firm paces before they cover: the others all stand fast until you give the word

March.

At which word the whole of the centre and left files will fall back and cover their right files: the whole to dress by their right, and to have their heels two inches apart. You will now give the word,

To your right prove distance of files;

At which word of command, the whole extend their right arms, with the points of their swords towards their right hand men, and the backs of the swords to the front; having proved their distance to the right, give the word,

Slope Swords.

You will now prove distance to the front, give the word,

To your front prove distance of files.

The whole of the front files stand fast, the centre and rear files extend the sword arm strait to the front; having proved distance, give the word,

Slope Swords,

Which being done, you may proceed to perform the six divisions of movements, either by fugle men, or word of command, as before shewn.

—

Method preparing to perform the Six Divisions of Movements on Horseback.

—

THE same instructions to be observed by the fugle men, for the performance of it on horseback as on foot. The drill will be fell in a rank entire, and told off exactly the same as when on foot, right, centre and left; but besides that, the drill must be told off in four divisions, upon a supposition of the four squadrons of the regiment, until such time as the whole of the regiment performs it, when there will be further necessity for it; this dividing them into four divisions, is a preparation for performing it with speed, which will be explained hereafter; neither will there be any necessity of easing files as when on foot, for if the men have their usual distance of files, which is eight inches from knee to knee, when the centre and left files fall back, there will be plenty of room; yet it will be necessary to prove their distance of files, for fear of an accident, which is done on horseback the same as on foot, with this difference, that in proving distance of files on horseback, the men stand well upon their stirrups.

After having drawn their swords, the same words of command will be made use of as when on foot; but when the pivets on the right fall back, they will take care to have no more than half a horse's length from the one in front from them; your files having doubled, you proceed to perform the sword exercise, either by word of command, or by fugle men; but it must always be observed, both on foot and on horseback, that the men remain perfectly steady when at position of *slope swords*, between every division of movements.

N. B. When the sword exercise is performed by fugle men, either on horseback, or on foot, after the word *first division*, &c. is given, a pause of about three seconds must be made before the sword is brought to the *prepare to guard*.

—

The Meaning of the Six Divisions of Movements explained.

—

The use of the first division of moments are upon a supposition of advancing; the use of the six cuts, *left and right protect*, are exactly the same as explained in the explanation of the drill motions. It contains sixteen motions.

Second Division explained.

The use of the second division of movements, are upon a supposition of retreating; the commencement and cuts are exactly the same as the first division; the guards and cuts to the rear are also explained in the drill motions. It contains fifteen motions.

Third Division explained.

The use of the third division of movements, is also upon a supposition of advancing, and is nearly the same as the first, with this difference, that there are four cuts more than in the first, three to cut the horse's head, and one to cut the man, and two guards in it for the protection of the horse's head. This division of movements must be done much quicker than any of the others, as it is much the longest, otherwise the ground would not do. It contains twenty-two motions.

Fourth Division explained.

The sole intention of this division of movements, is an attack against infantry. Having come to your guard, you are upon a supposition that an infantry man is kneeling with charged bayonet against you; you therefore immediately prepare to parry the bayonet off with the back of the sword; having parried, you instantly cut at the man with cut *two*, in such direction as to cut him under the hat; as soon as you have cut two, the sword must be brought to the position of Saint George, to be in readiness to cut one on the other side of you; and in all cuts in the infantry movements, the sword must be brought to the position of Saint George, as it stands to reason, the greater height a man cuts from, the more force he cuts with. You next give point to the right and left, not in the same direction as if fighting a man on horseback, but downwards, as supposing a man lying on the ground. You next cut three and four, and in cutting three, you must take care to carry the sword well round the head, and cut strong up to the front in both these last cuts. It must always be observed in the infantry cuts, that in cutting two and one, after the strength of the cuts are made, the back of the sword must be turned towards the horse's crup[40]; also in cutting three and four, that the sword is carried strait out to the front, in order to save the horse's head; for if a horse gets one cut, it makes him ever after shy. It contains fifteen motions.

Fifth Division explained.

This division of movements is on a supposition of fighting two men, or rather how to attack on either side of you; you therefore begin the attack on the near or left side of you, by cutting one and two at your antagonist, instantly bringing the sword round your head at the guard, and turning the body well to the right, you cut one and two again, and bring the sword to prepare to guard, then

---

40 "CROUP [of a *Horse*] the hindermost Part of a Horse, the Buttocks and Tail, from the Haunch Bones to the Dock." Nathan Bailey, *An Universal Etymological English Dictionary* (London: J. Buckland, W. Strahan, J.F. and C. Rivington, 1782).

give point to the left, then to the right, and in giving point to the right, the instant, you give point, the edge of the sword must be turned to the front, and the head to the left; you now cut five and six, guard and slope sword. This division contains fourteen motions.

Sixth Division explained.

This division which is the last, is an attack on the right, and defence to the left; the supposition is that you are attacking a man on the right of you. First give point to the right, then cut one at your antagonist's back of his head, instantly turning your sword you cut at his face with cut two, and bring the sword with the hilt against your left shoulder, point upwards, ready to parry; you will act the defensive part, by first parrying the point off which is given to the right; having parried, you instantly bring the sword back to the first position of the parry, to be in readiness to guard the cut which is made at the back of your head; having guarded the back of your head, you next guard your face, then give point to the front, prepare to guard, guard, then slope swords. This division contains twelve motions.

Your men having performed the six divisions of movement, standing and formed to their former front, it is next to be performed in speed; it has already been mentioned also that your drills are to be told off in four divisions. You will therefore proceed as follows: *Ranks by threes from your center outwards. Wheel. March. Halt. Dress.* The two left hand divisions will wheel to their left, and the two right hand divisions to their right by threes. You will next give the word

March.

At which word of command the whole move strait forward, until they come to the ground appointed at each end for the leading threes to wheel, *i. e.* the leading three of the left half rank wheels to the right, and the leading three of the right half rank wheels to the left; then they move forward in that direction until the divisions that are in the rear of both half ranks come upon their grounds appointed, where they will be ordered to *Halt*, and *Wheel up*, the front divisions keep moving on, till they get about thirty yards off those divisions that are halted, then they *Halt* and *Wheel up*. You will have your men in two divisions, at each end of your ground, formed opposite each other; you will next give the word,

Perform the Sword Exercise in speed,

At which word of command, the right and left hand men of each division move forward one horse length, and wait there until the word, *First division* is given; as soon that word is given, they will start off in speed, go through their division, and form up in the proper pieces in the rear of those divisions that were opposite them; as soon as one man has started, the next must forward a horse's length, and so on until they have all gone off. The second man will go off with the second, the third with the third, the fourth with the fourth, the fifth with the fifth, and the sixth man with the sixth division; and should there be more than six men in each of your-divisions, as there will be, when the whole squadron comes to act, the seventh man starts with the first, the eighth man with the second, and so on until the whole of your men are gone off. The men having all done one division of movements and formed up, the next thing to be done is the attack and defence standing, and in order to prepare for it, you will give the word,

Divisions wheel inwards. March.

At the word *march*, those divisions that belonged to the right half rank, wheel to their left, and those divisions of the left half rank, wheel to their right. *Halt. Dress.* You have one division of each half rank formed in the rear, which divisions are to act as the rear rank; you will now give the word,

>*Divisions to your center extend your files. March.*

At the word *march*, they will go off in a brisk trot, or a canter, casting their eye to the rear, and taking about two horse's lengths distance from the files in the rear of them, they will halt and front, the files in the rear taking care to cover those in the front; you will now give the word,

>*Rear rank move forward to the attack. March.*

At this word of command, the rear rank moves forward and attacks the front rank, and goes back to their places; you will next give the word,

>*Front rank, to your right about, turn. Move forward to the attack.*
>*March.*

At the word *march*, they will go and attack the rear rank, and come back to the ground they went from.

The Attack and Defence Standing Explained.

As soon as the rear rank are ordered to move forward to the attack, and have got the word *march*, (they advance a few paces) come to the *prepare to guard*, then *guard*. The front rank will come to the guard of *bridle arm protect*. The rank now comes up, 1st, Gives point to the right. 2nd, Cuts at the back of the head. 3rd, At the face. 4th, Horse's head near side. 5th, Horse's head off side. 6th, At the inside of the man's face. 7th, Guards against cut three.

8th, Cuts at his thigh, and walks off, protecting his bridle arm. Dressing by the center, when come on their ground, halt and front.

The front rank having come to the guard of *bridle arm protect*, as soon as they see their antagonists preparing to give point, they will prepare to parry; 1st, Parry. 2nd, Guard the back of the head. 3rd, Guard the face. 4th, Horse near side protect. 5th, Off side protect. 6th, Guard the inside of the face. 7th, Cut three. 8th, Guard the thigh. 9th, Cut six. The front having gone about, and ordered to attack the rear rank, they will, at the word *march*, also advance a few paces, and then come to their guard regular, each rear rank man taking the time from his front rank man for doing the same. The front rank now comes up and begins the attack on the off side: 1st, Cut at his horse's head off side, 2nd, Inside of the man's face. 3rd, Guards against cut three. 4th, Cuts at his thigh. 5th, Guards against cut six. 6th, Cuts at his sword arm. 7th, At his bridle arm. 8th, Gives point to the right. 9th, Cuts at the back of the head. 10th, At his face. 11th, At his horse's head near side, and walks off, protecting his sword arm. The rear rank will first guard the horse's head off side. 2nd, Inside of the face. 3rd. Cut three. 4th, Guard the thigh. 5th, Cut six. 6th, Guard sword arm. 7th, Bridle arm, 8th, Parry. 9th, Guard the back of the head. 10th, Guard the face. 11th, Horse near side protect, then as the front rank walks off, cut six at his sword arm.

The front and rear rank having attacked each other standing, it is next to be performed in speed: you will therefore prepare for it, by giving the word of command,

To your outward Flanks close your Files. March.

Your men being formed into divisions again, you will wheel them backwards by going about by threes, the divisions that belong to the left half rank on their right backwards, and the divisions that belong to the right half rank on their left backwards;

The Attack and Defence in speed. March.

At the word *march*, the two men that are on the right of the right hand division, belonging to the left half rank, will go off in a canter, when got about ten yards of the next two, and so on until the whole are gone off; the left hand division of the left half rank taking care to occupy the ground time enough that the right hand division went from, and as soon as the two first men that went off are got to the left flank of the left division belonging to the right half rank which they must run to, they will pull up their horses and walk slowly on, till the whole are come up, when they will walk out and go and form on the same ground, where they performed the six divisions of movements standing, each man taking care to get into his proper place, whilst he is in the rear of the right half rank. As soon as the whole of the men of the left half rank are clear of the flank of the left division of the right half rank, the right half rank will commence the attack, beginning the attack from the left of their left division, the right hand division taking care to occupy their ground soon enough; and when the two first men that went off are come to the ground where the left half rank went from, they will also pull up, and follow the same instructions given for the left half rank, then walk out and form in their place.

—

Motions of the Attack and Defence in Speed explained.

—

The right hand man of the two, always when they start, must be rather in the front, with his sword hand at his left shoulder, ready to parry the point off that is made at him; the man who attacks comes up on the near side; 1st, Gives point to the right. 2nd. Cuts at the back of the head. 3rd, Cuts at his face. 4th, Cuts at his

No. 1. *Ring Post.*

No. 1. *Ring Post ex-plained.*

A. The part that fastens in the ground.

B. The center piece that slides up and down.

C. The top of the center piece, made stronger than the other part, to support the ring iron.

D. A hole bored to put the ring iron in.

E. Iron straps nailed on the standing piece to keep the center piece ready.

F. A bolt made to keep the center piece to its proper height.

N. B. This is the properest post to be made use of, as the height can be varied.

No. 2. *Ring Post.*

No. 2. *Ring Post ex-plained.*

A. The post about four inches square.

B. The top of the post, about 7 feet from the ground.

C. A hole bored in the post for the iron to go in.

D. The iron about ½ inch thick, 18 inches high, and 2 feet projection.

E. A hole punched near the end of the iron for the hook F.

F. A hook made to turn round in E, with the point a little raised.

G. The ring is made flat, is 5 inches over, about ½ inch thick, and is about ¼ of an inch in the flat.

horse's head near side and rides on, guarding his sword arm, and bringing the sword round to the rear, as he sees the other advancing on him, when he will now prepare to parry, and be attacked in the same manner, as explained. The defensive part is, 1st, Parry the point off. 2nd, Guard the back of the head. 3rd, Guard the face. 4th, Horse near side protect, and cut six.

—

OF PRACTICAL MOTIONS.

—

THE men having performed the attack and defence in speed, the next thing to be done, is to give point to the right and left at the ring. There should be a ring post and ring for each division. The divisions are to be formed about thirty yards from the ring posts they are to run at, the right hand man always taking care to advance one horse's length in front of the division.

They will set off in a canter, and increase their pace as they approach the ring. Come to *prepare to guard*; then *guard*; then come to the position of *front give point*, resting the sword firmly on the peak of their helmets, drawing the sword hand well back, and looking stedfastly at the ring, taking care to have their left shoulders well up to the front; they will give point strong, and immediately guard their sword arm, as we now suppose they are giving point to the right. They will ride about thirty or forty yards on the other side of the post, where they will form up in their proper places, fronting the posts. They will next give point to the left; the same instructions with respect to starting, &c. as in giving point to the right, with this difference, that after giving point to the left, they guard their bridle arm instead of their sword arm, taking care always to look the way they guard.

OF GIVING EDGE, OR PROVING CUT 5 AND 6, CAVALRY MOVEMENTS,

—

The next thing to be done after running at the ring, is giving edge. The ring irons are to be taken down, and sticks about six inches in length put in the holes of the posts were the ring irons were fixed, with a potatoe on the top of each stick; the right hand men advance a horse's length the same as mentioned before, and go off in a canter, increasing their pace as they approach the post; they will come to the *prepare to guard*, then guard; will make a feint of cut five, instantly cut six strong at the potatoe, and immediately after the cut six, guard their sword arm, ride on about thirty or forty yards on the other side of the post, and form up again fronting the post, and having proved cut six, will return and prove cut five, making a feint of cut six, and cutting five strong at the potatoe, taking care, as soon as they have made the cut, to guard their bridle arm. Having proved cut five and six, cavalry movements, they will proceed to prove the infantry cuts, which is done as follows:

—

OF GIVING EDGE, INFANTRY MOVEMENTS.

—

The starting, &c. the same as already mentioned. Having come to the position of *guard*, they will come to the position of *on the right to the front parry*, and just before they come to the post, they will parry, and instantly cut (two) at the potatoe, bring the sword to the position of St. George, and when come opposite to the other post, cut (one) and bring the sword to the position of the *prepare to guard*, ride on about thirty or forty yards, and form up as before-mentioned; they will return by cutting (three) at the first post, and cutting four at the second; after cutting three, the sword must be brought to position of St. George, and after cutting four, to the *prepare to guard:* for in the infantry cuts, the men are never to guard themselves after they make a cut.

—

HOW THE POSTS ARE TO BE FIXED TO PROVE INFANTRY CUTS.

—

There is nothing better for this business, than two picquet posts, with holes bored in the top of them to put the sticks in; but if you have none, you must have posts about four feet six inches long; they must be drove down about seven paces from each other, not in a direct line, but one to be fixed about one pace and an half to the left of the other, at the extent of those seven paces.

E N D.

DONALD MCALPINE

During the year 1769, in Boston, Massachusetts, a teenage boy named Benjamin Thompson enrolled in a local fencing school. Thompson had been born in nearby Middlesex County, and had taken up residence in Boston for the purpose of apprenticing to a dry goods dealer. He would one day marry into an aristocratic family and become the famous Sir Benjamin Thompson, Count Rumford, best known today for his work as a physicist, and for his contributions to the then burgeoning field of thermodynamics. During his youth, however, Thompson unwittingly made another contribution to history, that, up until now, has been known to few.[1] While taking lessons in swordsmanship, he recorded some elementary fencing instructions, and included an accompanying sketch. Today, this drawing is currently the earliest known illustration of fencing technique set down in the American colonies. During the nineteenth century, the diary containing the drawings was bequeathed to Joseph B. Walker, of Concord, New Hampshire, who was a descendant of Thompson's first wife. At this time, the diary was described as

> a very interesting and suggestive relic...which is very significant of the tastes and occupations of his youth. It is a memorandum-book of substantial linen paper, with parchment cover and a brass clasp, some leaves of which have been cut out, thirty-six of those it may have originally contained being still left...The contents of the book are, as will be seen, very miscellaneous, giving tokens of the bent of genius of the youth, with anticipatory hints of the characteristics and occupations of his mature life.[2]

This diary eventually found its way into the hands of the New Hampshire Historical Society, where it resides today.

The originator of these techniques—that is, Thompson's teacher —was Donald McAlpine, a native of Scotland, who first came to Boston in 1769 with "Captain Gorham from Nova Scotia."[3] Previously, McAlpine had served as Sergeant in Captain Archibald Campbell's Company in the 78th Regiment of Foot during the French and Indian War (or Seven Years War), until being discharged in 1763. This regiment, known as "Fraser's Highlanders," had been raised in Inverness, Scotland in 1757, by Lieutenant-Colonel Simon Fraser of Lovat, son of the notorious Jacobite Simon "the Fox" Fraser, 18th Chief of the Clan Fraser of Lovat. The younger Simon Fraser, at his father's bidding, led the Frasers in the service of "Bonny Prince Charlie" Charles Edward Stewart in 1745, but was not among those forces sent to take part in the disastrous battle of Culloden. Following the failed rebellion, after spending time on the run, Fraser raised a new regiment in Scotland, obtained a commission from the British as Lieutenant-

Sir Benjamin Thompson Rumford, pictured in his *Memoirs*.

Colonel, and embarked for America in 1757 with the young Donald McAlpine. The attire of these soldiers was described as follows:

The uniform was the full Highland dress, with musquet and broad sword, to which many of the soldiers added the dirk at their own expence, and a purse of badger's or otter's skin. The bonnet was raised or cocked on one side, with a slight bend inclining down to the right ear, over which were suspended two or more black feathers. Eagle's or hawk's feathers were usually worn by the gentlemen, in the Highlands, while the bonnets of the common people were ornamented with a bunch of the distinguishing mark of the clan or district. The ostrich feathers in the bonnets of the soldiers were a modern addition of that period, as the present load of plumage on the bonnet is a still more recent introduction, forming, however, in hot climates, a good defence against a vertical sun.[4]

During the war, Fraser's Highlanders fought with distinction at the Siege of Louisbourg, the Battle of the Plains of Abraham, and the capture of Montreal. Of his own service, McAlpine later related that, being "actuated by the strictest Principles of Loyalty from his Infancy," he

embark'd in the Cause of the British Government & Constitution in the Year 1757, & served His Majesty with the distinguished Character of a good Soldier & Officer in the 78th Regiment of Highlanders commanded by Col. Symen Fraser in his dift. Routes in North America during the War before the last. That your Memorialist at the Conclusion of that War remained in the Country, where he acquired a comfortable Fortune...[5]

In another account, McAlpine claimed to have served "with some reputation in the 78th Regiment of Highlanders."[6]

Several years after the end of the war, in 1769, McAlpine arrived in Boston from Nova Scotia. Almost immediately, he set up a fencing school, and announced its existence in a local newspaper:

BOSTON, 25th *November*, 1769.

To the Lovers of the noble Science of D E F E N C E.

GENTLEMEN who chuse to be instructed in the Art commonly called the BACK SWORD, are desired to apply to *Donald Mᶜ Alpine*, formerly Serjeant in the 78th Regiment, who will instruct them in said Science to their entire Satisfaction, for *Ten Shillings Sterling* per Month, at his Room in Mr. CARNE's House, near the *Meeting House, New Boston*, from Hours of One, until Five in the Evening.

N. B. Any Gentlemen who chuse to be instructed in said Science privately, may be waited upon by applying to said *Mc Alpine*. —— He can likewise instruct Ladies and Gentlemen in the FRENCH Language, in the most concise manner, and on the most reasonable Terms. DONALD MᶜALPINE[7]

This was, as previously noted, the same year that the young Benjamin Thompson entered his school as a scholar. The "Meeting House" which McAlpine mentions as the site of his Boston fencing school was the West Church at Lynde and Cambridge Streets.[8]

During the first few years of its existence, McAlpine's school changed locations several times. In April of 1770 he was teaching in the bustling center of "New Boston," out of "the Lane opposite *Ebenezer Storer*'s Warehouse in Union-Street, where Gentlemen

From the *Boston Post-Boy*, December 6, 1773.

The site of McAlpine's Boston school: The Green Dragon Tavern, after a 1773 watercolor. Reproduced in *The Lodge of Saint Andrew* (Boston: 1870).

may be taught to their entire Satisfaction."[9] In early 1771, he had moved to a house "near the Mill-Bridge, and leading down to the New Mills."[10] Later that year he was teaching at the popular Green Dragon Tavern on Union Street, where he warned his students that "they must begin [instruction] very soon, as [McAlpine] has a Call to teach in another Town, and this Quarter is the last he intends to teach in Boston."[11] He had returned to the city, however, by 1773, when he announced that he would once again teach the backsword at "the Green Draggon Tavern."[12] The next January, McAlpine secured an additional student in the person of Bostonian Thomas Newell, who wrote in his diary: "This evening entered to McCalpen to learn the back sword."[13] In 1775, McAlpine's school was located beneath the "the Sign of the Two Gladiators", presumably a semi-permanent work space, on the north side of King Street (now State Street) near the Long Wharf.[14]

McAlpine's career as a master-of-arms—and indeed, his entire life—was turned upside down by the outbreak of the American

Sign of the Green Dragon Tavern, reproduced in *The Lodge of Saint Andrew*.

Revolution in April of 1775, commencing with the local battles of Lexington, Concord, and Bunker Hill. After this time, Boston became an enclave of British troops and loyalists, surrounded by besieging colonial forces led by General George Washington. Following the outbreak of hostilities, McAlpine unhesitatingly sided with British forces. Speaking of himself in the third person, he related:

> [At] the Beginning of the last unhappy War, he then quitting his Property & Family (of old & infirm Father & Mother in Law, a Wife & 5 Children) took the earliest Opportunity of serving his King & Country to support the Rebellion, & Join'd His Maj's Forces commanded by Genl. Gage at Boston in 1775, from which Time he continued in the service with unwearied Assiduity & Perseverance in dift. Quarters of America...[15]

An associate of McAlpine's later recounted that "I Knew Mr. McAlpine previous to the war, that he joined the King's Army at

> TO all LOVERS of the NOBLE SCIENCE of DE-
> FENCE, Commonly Called the BACK SWORD
> who incline to be instructed in that Art, are desired to
> apply to DONALD McALPINE, at the Sign of the
> Two Gladiators, North Side King Street, Near the
> Long Wharff, where he attends from Ten o'Clock be-
> fore Noon till One, and from Three after Noon till
> Sunset. Any Gentlemen who chuse to be instructed
> privately may be waited upon as they and the Master
> shall agree. Any Gentlemen inclining to encourage
> said McAlpine, to leave their Names at the Shop of
> Mr. William McAlpine Stationer, in Marlborough
> Street, Corner of Bromfield's Lane.
> N B. When there is a sufficient Number, School to
> be opened immediately.

One of McAlpine's last known advertisements, from the *Boston News-Letter*, December 28, 1775.

Boston & did duty there as a volunteer while the Town was block-aded."[16] In a more detailed account of this period, McAlpine explained that

> his Loyalty to his sovereign & his attachment to his native Country added to the resentments those principles created against him in the natives of America obliged him to leave his property his family an aged & infirm father & mother in Law, a wife & seven Children & to join General Gage at Boston in the summer of the same year; That he continued in Boston untill its evacuation when he accompanied the Troops untill their arrival at New York where he enlisted for the King's service 85 men & was appointed a Captain in Major Stark's Corps & after that he joined the Queens Rangers & had a considerable share of that hard & severe service for which that Corps was not less distinguished than for their spirit & Gallantry...[17]

This last-mentioned unit in which McAlpine served, the Queen's Rangers, was the successor to Robert Roger's Rangers, and would go on to become legendary in the history of the

A Rifleman of the Queen's Rangers, after a water colour by James Murray.
Courtesy of the Toronto Public Library.

American War of Independence. Today, the Queen's Rangers are
regarded by many as one of the first Special Forces units to operate
in North America. The eighty-five volunteers raised by McAlpine
served in the New Hampshire Volunteers, which was disbanded in
May of 1777, and absorbed into the Queen's Rangers, at which
time McAlpine replaced John Eagles as captain. In September, the
unit's soldiers distinguished themselves at the Battle of Brandy-

wine, where they suffered many casualties while attacking entrenched American positions. At this time, McAlpine resigned as captain.[18] He was back in New Hampshire in 1778, when local loyalist Enos Stevens recorded that "Capt McAlpian came for to instruct the gentlemen the broad sword &c. I enterd as one of his scollars at the rate of one guinea per month. Now the chief of our exercise is in the school."[19]

The major theatre of the American war soon moved to the southern portion of the country, and along with it went Donald McAlpine. He was soon "appointed Captain in the South Carolina Rangers By Lord Rawdon,"[20] and later absorbed into the Royal North Carolina Regiment, wherein he served as a lieutenant in Captain Daniel McNiell's company.[21] McAlpine himself recounted:

> In the year 1781 being then a captain in the South Carolina rangers [I] had the misfortune in an Action with the Enemy to be severely wounded in several places & to be taken prisoner & continued several months prisoner...[22]

In another more detailed account of this incident, McAlpine explained:

> That your Memorialist in the year 1781 being Captn. in the So. Carolina Rangers, & at a Time in a Covering Party on the Congarese in that Province, had the Misfortune to be wounded in sevl. Places, a Couple of Balls now lodged in his Body, to the great Prejudice of his Welfare & Loss of the use of his Left arm, was then taken Prisoner & stript of every Thing, even to the very bloody Shirt on his Back, plundered of his Baggage & many Articles purchased for the Use of the Regiment, continued as Prisoner from the 23rd Feby. to the summer following, then exchanged in Charlestown, & when the South Carolina Rangers were drafted into the So. Carolina Regiment, he joined Col. Hamilton's Regiment as Lieut. and continued untill it was reduced.[23]

From April to June 24, 1782, still recovering from his wounds, McAlpine served in Lieutenant Colonel John Hamilton's Company of the Royal North Carolina Regiment.[24]

McAlpine's loyalty to the King would cost his family dearly. Following the end of the war, he stated in his pension application that

> he has in England a wife & two children with him to support; that his Children in America also want Assistance but he finds it totally impracticable to support himself & family here much less to afford assistance to them there therefore considering his long services, zeal & Loyalty his former losses & present distresses he prays that you would afford him some present support to relieve himself & family from their present distress he having nothing but his half pay as Lieut. to depend upon. And your memorialist as in duty bound will ever pray...[25]

In his application, McAlpine included a vast list of property items which he had lost as a result of the war, including an "elegant House," all the furniture and belongings it contained, fifteen thousand pounds, "1200 Acres of Land," a herd of cattle, his library of books, "two Dragoon Horses", a "Dragoon Sword," and one "Pair Pistols." Also listed were one "Negro Man, by Trade a Bricklayer, 18 Years of age," and "a Negro Woman, a complete Washer, Ironer and Cook."[26]

McAlpine's pension application contained numerous testimony from friends and associates—including his former major in the Rangers, John Harrison. Another, Abijah Willard, stated that "I always esteemed [McAlpine] a good & loyal subject and that he was zealous & active in assisting the Kings Cause." Stephen Holland claimed that McAlpine was "always esteemed...a good and loyal Subject when he was in New Hampshire, and [I] have always understood since, that he has continued to persevere in the same line of conduct." His former commandant, Lieutenant-Colonel Hamilton, testified that "McAlpine has ever behaved himself as a very gallant & spirited Officer."[27] Nor was McAlpine forgotten by his now-illustrious former fencing student. Among the supporters of McAlpine's claim was listed one "Sir Benjamin Thompson No. 8 St. Albans Street."[28] During the Revolution, Thompson had served as major in the New Hampshire loyalist militia, and advised both General Gage and Lord George Germain.

The testimony was likely helpful to McAlpine's family, but not to the old soldier himself. On January 25, 1789, McAlpine "died of the Wounds he received in the Province of South Carolina on his Majestys Service." Following his death, his former Lieutenant-Colonel wrote,

> I...Certify that Mrs. McAlpine has three Small orphan Children & by the death of her Husband Capt. McAlpine is deprived of all annual income & is destitute of Support for her self & Family. I do therefore most Humbly but most Earnestly recommend her to the Humane attention of the Board of Commissioners as an object truly Worthy of their Benevolence & attention for Temporary Support.[29]

MCALPINE'S METHOD

Little evidence survives pertaining to the techniques taught by Donald McAlpine. However, given the significance of McAlpine's place in American fencing history, a brief look is merited.

Directions for the Back-Sword —

1st. To put Yourself in a proper posture of Defence — Viz.t — hold your Sword firm in your Right hand with your point Elevated as high as your Antagonist's head & your Hilt a little Depressed bringing your sword to range with your Ant.s body and with his Eyes, then Step forward with your right foot. about A foot forming a square with Your two feet then Stand upright & take your distance Just so as to touch your Ant.s Breast then bend your left Knee which will bring your body in a proper Posture of Defence — from M.r McAlpine. —

McAlpine's "Directions for the Back-Sword," as transcribed and illustrated by Thompson. *Courtesy of the New Hampshire Historical Society.*

Following are McAlpine's "directions" as transcribed by his student, Sir Benjamin Thompson Rumford:

> Directions for the Back-Sword: I. To put yourself in a proper posture of Defence, viz., hold your Sword firm in your Right hand, with your point elevated as high as your Antagonist's head, and your hilt a little depressed, bringing your sword to range with your Antagonist's body and with his eyes: then step forward with your right foot about a foot, forming a square with your two feet: then stand upright and take your distance, just so as to touch your Antagonist's breast: then bend your left knee, which will bring your body in a proper Posture of Defence.[30]

These directions (taking one's distance) are consistent with fencing techniques that are still taught to this day, and Thompson's sketches of the combatants' postures resembles illustrations in Scottish backsword treatises of the period, such as those written by William Hope and Donald McBane.

And this would be all that is known of McAlpine's method, were it not for another student of his, named Robert Hewes. Unlike his fencing master, Hewes would side with American rebel forces, and become a member of the secret revolutionary society, the Sons of Liberty. According to Hewes himself, his training in fencing began about 1770 in Boston. In 1798, Hewes offered to teach "*the manly exercise of the Broad Sword*, in the true Highland stile, as taught by the late famous *Donald Mc Alpin.*"[31] In 1808, Hewes further recounted:

> I do understand what the Broad Sword is scientifically; having learnt it of the famous DONALD Mc GILPIN, a Scotch Highlander, above thirty eight years ago; and I have had the honor and pleasure of teaching it to many of the Officers of our Revolutionary Army, in Roxbury and Cambridge, in the year 1775—and have done it at times, ever since.[32]

Detail of Thompson's illustration. *Courtesy of the New Hampshire Historical Society.*

In 1809, Hewes provided the following information about the method of using the broadsword that he had learned from McAlpine:

IT always has been, and with some is still a disputed point which is best, the Broad Sword, or Small Sword.—Some will assert, (not knowing what the true Scotch Broad Sword is) that the Broad Sword is no manner of Defence against the Small Sword.—Others (who understand the Broad Sword well, and can play well, by daily experience) prove, that it is a complete Defence against the Small Sword, by evading or guarding their thrusts—and cutting their head or arm, which they generally do twice out of three:—the reason is, being too much practised in bending the elbow the Cuts of the Broad Sword meet their arm instantly;—as was verified the other day thus:—One of my Scholars introduced a French Gentleman and desired to play the Small Sword with him. We played loose pretty sharp a few moments, and neither hit.—He then desired us to play Cut and Thrust—we did;—but he no sooner moved than I cut his arm three times. He then says to my Scholar the reason Mr. HEWES cut my arm so easy is, because I am too much in the habit of playing the Small Sword with a crooked arm—therefore I cannot play Cut and Thrust. This Gentleman was candid enough to own, that the Cut and Thrust cannot be played with a crooked arm:—Therefore, to play true and with safety with a Cut and Thrust, the Broad Sword, according to the Scotch and Austrian systems, must be well learnt.—Which forbids the bending the elbow, raising or lowering the arm or passing the line to the right or left—in fine, the arms is as an iron bar, the wrist the pivot round which the Sabre flies, or in other words, the hand and hilt of the Sword is the centre of action, as a hob to a wheel; the blade as the spokes.[33]

The same year, Hewes engaged in a contest with a French rival, in which the combatants used "broad sword Foils." Of this incident, Hewes recounted:

To Mr. Millet.

SIR—In last Saturday's *Centinel*, you charge me with saying, that you know nothing of Fencing, &c—and invite me to a public trial of skill, &c—As to the scurrilous charge of my saying that you know nothing of the use of the Sword, I can in conscience deny it: —But, what I have said, and do now say, is this—That I believe you understand the Small Sword very well; but that you do not so well understand the Broad Sword;—so think some of your friends.

Mr. MILLET, you must give me leave to presume, that I do understand what the Broad Sword is scientifically; having learnt it of the famous DONALD Mc GILPIN, a Scotch Highlander, above thirty eight years ago; and I have had the honor and pleasure of teaching it to many of the Officers of our Revolutionary Army, in *Roxbury* and *Cambridge*, in the year 1775—and have done it at times, ever since. During the last ten years I have kept a regular school. But the Broad Sword you understand, is the French Counterpoint—a great difference.

The next thing is you invite me to a publick trial of skill.—With whom? A man I do not know. And for what? Why to please you, and a gaping multitude, that will know no more of the merits of it after it is over, than they did before it commenced.—What I, the hoary head, in boyish martial sports, on publick stage exposed! Oh, no no! Mr. MILLET; my rank in society, my age, forbid it; especially with a competitor I do not know. But why do you want another trial, when we have already had a fair one, by your own application and desire; and contrary to my wish; yet I desire to be thankful it was so public that I have sufficient evidence to full substantiate the merits of our combat.— A plain recital of the facts, attested by the evidence with a technical description of our combat, I will endeavor to relate in truth and dispassionately;—

About a month ago, you was introduced to me by your friend, Mr. ————. After being in the room a little while, you desired to play with me—I declined. There were two young gentlemen, my scholars, in the room—I pointed to the eldest of them, and said, "Play with him."

"Yes," said the young gentleman, "I will play with you."

(MILLET.) "No," said you, "if I play with any body here, I shall play with the master."

"Then," said I, "you'll play with me, quick time."

I then presented you with one broad sword Foil; I having the other myself. My two pupils paid strict attention to everything we did; but your friend, Mr. P————, seemed to be regardless of what was going on, for he sat all the time eating nuts as hearty as a grey squirrel.

Now comes the technical description of the combat:—First, we join issue upon an inside guard—I cut you with cut two, on the outside of your arm:—you then come to the counterpoint guard in seconde—I cut you four, under your arm;—we join again and I cut your leg with cut six;—the next was a counter.

I then said, "Come, Mr. MILLET, attack me in your turn, and do it well, or I shall catch you." You then made a little movement and hit my arm. You then came in a very swordsman like manner, and made cut five, at my body—I spring back, slipped your cut, and gave you a plump cut upon the head—and so the combat finished, by my cutting you four times, and you cutting me once.

Now, Mr. MILLET, since you have treated me in this scurrilous manner, by denying the merits of our combat, which was solicited by yourself, and persisting in publishing your scurrilous piece; I am determined never to have another trial of skill with you, publick or private; nor to have any altercation or conversation with you, written or verbal; and if any thing more shall appear in the papers, I am determined not to take the least notice of it.

> ROBERT HEWES,

Jan 25, 1808.

[The two gentlemen scholars of Mr. H. have appeared at this office, and testified to the truth of Mr. H's account of the combat, above referred to.] [34]

In a 1799 advertisement Hewes further stated that with his "system of defence...a person attacked can defend himself against the Small Sword, Broad Sword, Sabre, Gun and Bayonet, cane or small Stick of Wood." [35] Later notices by Hewes added the "spaderoon," "Claymoor," and "rapier," to the list of weapons taught, and the "boarding pike" to the weapons which his cane defense method was capable of defending against. [36] An avid collector of fencing treatises (his bookshelf contained Angelo's, among others), Hewes later claimed to have united the "Scotch, Austrian, French and English methods into one system." [37] In 1811, however, he was still offering to teach "the true Highland Broad Sword, or Art of Attack and Defence, as practised by the Scotch Highlanders..." [38] In 1825, only a few years before his death, he referred to "the true Scotch Highland Broad Sword, called the Andrew Farrara, Claymoor..." [39] In one of his more humorous advertisements, Hewes quoted a certain Scot, in a passage which may possibly be regarded as a final tribute to his old teacher:

Mr. H. does not profess mountbankery, such as "taking out the button from your shirt collar, without cutting your throat,"— (English)—or "spleeting a mon doone from the shoulder to the seidle at one cut"—(Scotch)—or taking a man's head off at one cut as easy as you would a poppy or onion-stalk"—(Lady Mary Montegue's Janizaries)—but he professes to teach the art to prevent the buttons from being taken from the shirt collar, or being thus cut down, or the head thus easily taken off.[40]

---

1 This author first wrote about Thompson's sketches nine years ago, in an article for the journal of the Association of Historical Fencing. See Ben Miller, "Fencing in Colonial America and the Early Republic: 1620 – 1800," *Estafilade*, New York: 2009. (https://www.ahfi.org/wp-content/uploads/library/estafilade_fencing-in-america.pdf)

2 George Edward Ellis, *Memoir of Sir Benjamin Thompson, Count Rumford, with notices of his daughter* (Boston: Estes and Lauriat, 1871), 26.

3 *A Report of the Record Commissioners of the City of Boston, containing the Selectmen's minutes from 1769 through April, 1775* (Boston: Rockwell and Churchill, 1893), 47.

4 Colonel David Stewart, *Sketches of the Character, Manners, and Present State of the Highlanders of Scotland: with Details of the Military Service of the Highland Regiments. Vol. 2* (Edinburgh: Archibald Constable & Co., 1822), 66-67.

5 Great Britain, Public Record Office, Audit Office, Class 13, Volume 131, folio 82.

6 Ibid., folio 92.

7 *Boston Chronicle*, Nov 27, 1769.

8 Seybolt, Robert Francis, *The Private Schools of Colonial Boston* (Cambridge, Mass.: Harvard University Press, 1935), 60.

9 *Boston Gazette*, April 9, 1770.

10 *Boston Gazette*, February 11, 1771.

11 *Boston News Letter*, October 3, 1771.

12 *Boston Post-Boy*, December 6, 1773.

13 *Proceedings of the Massachusetts Historical Society, Vol. XV* (Boston: Published by the Society, 1878), 347.

14 *Boston News Letter*, December 28, 1775.

15 Great Britain, Public Record Office, Audit Office, Class 13, Volume 131,

folio 82.

16 Ibid., folio 95.

17 Ibid., folio 92.

18 Thomas A. Murray, *Gregor McKinnon*, March 5, 2010. (http://www.uelac.org/Loyalist-Info/extras/McKinnon-Gregor/McKinnon-Gregor-by-Thomas-Murray.pdf)

19 Thomas Altherr, *Sports in North America: a Documentary History, Volume I, Part I* (Gulf Breeze, FL: Academic International Press, 1996), 154.

20 Great Britain, Public Record Office, Audit Office, Class 13, Volume 131, folio 93.

21 *Loyalists in the Southern Campaign of the Revolutionary War, Vol. 1* (Baltimore: Genealogical Publishing Co., 1981).

22 Great Britain, Public Record Office, Audit Office, Class 13, Volume 131, folio 92.

23 Ibid.

24 *Loyalists in the Southern Campaign of the Revolutionary War, Vol. 1* (Baltimore: Genealogical Publishing Co., 1981).

25 Great Britain, Public Record Office, Audit Office, Class 13, Volume 131, folio 92.

26 Ibid., folios 80, 83, 99-100.

27 Ibid., folios 93-95.

28 Ibid., folio 83.

29 Ibid., folio 113.

30 Ellis, 29-30.

31 *Columbian Centinel*, July 18, 1798.

32 *Columbian Centinel*, January 27, 1808.

33 *Columbian Centinel*, May 17, 1809.

34 *Columbian Centinel*, January 27, 1808.

35 *Constitutional Telegraph*, October 19, 1799.

36 *Columbian Centinel*, March 16, 1803.

37 *Boston Independent Chronicle*, September 22, 1814; *Columbian Centinel*, March 16, 1803.

38 *Boston Commercial Gazette*, November 21, 1811.

39 *Columbian Centinel*, Nov 26, 1825.

40 *Constitutional Telegraph*, October 19, 1799.

ABOUT THE CONTRIBUTORS

JARED KIRBY

Jared Kirby has been involved in Western Martial Arts and Combat for Screen & Stage for over 20 years. He teaches in New York City (and the metro area) and has choreographed fights Off-Broadway, Nationally, in London and Sydney.

As a Fight Coordinator, Jared has worked with stars such as Peter Sarsgaard, Steve Guttenberg, Cameron Douglas and has trained performers who are working on hit shows. Jared is a member of Actor's Equity and SAG/AFTRA.

He is the president of Combat Con in Las Vegas, past president of Art of Combat, and served for six years on the board of the International Order of the Sword & Pen.

Jared currently teaches fencing at SUNY Purchase, Sarah Lawrence College and is a Master of Arms (*Maestro d'Armi*) through the Martinez Academy of Arms. Jared has an ongoing Combat for Screen & Stage class in New York City and teaches at the prestigious Tom Todoroff Conservatory as well as the NY Conservatory for Dramatic Arts.

He teaches a variety of workshops across the US and around the world including Canada, England, Scotland, Finland, Italy and Australia. He has taught at the Paddy Crean International Art of the Sword Workshop, the International Swordfighting and Martial Arts Convention (ISMAC), Rapier Camp and the Western Washington WMA Workshop just to name a few.

Jared is the editor and one of the translators of *Italian Rapier Combat*, the first complete, professional translation of Capo Ferro. He is also the editor and wrote the introduction for *The School of Fencing* by Domenico Angelo and annotated by Maestro Jeannette Acosta-Martínez. Most recently *The Gentleman's Guide to Duelling* was released in February 2014 and a reprint of Donald McBane's *The Expert Swordsman's Companion* was released in January 2017. For more information, see Amazon.com.

PAUL MACDONALD

Maestro Paul Macdonald was born in 1972, and raised in the West Highland village of Glenuig, Moidart, Scotland. He began his study of fencing in 1992 at Napier University, Edinburgh, there founding and running the University club as President and principal instructor for two and a half years. With an ever-growing interest in historical swordsmanship, he founded the Dawn Duellists Society in 1994, and ran the DDS as President until 2006.

Since 1994, Maestro Macdonald has dedicated his path to European arms and martial arts, travelling throughout the UK, Europe, Canada and the US to research, study, practice, present seminars, demonstrations and teach. He has studied many styles of historical European combat and revived the methods and techniques of several lost systems, such as the medieval duelling shield, *spada in arme*, dusack and backsword. In 1998, Maestro Macdonald founded the British Federation for Historical Swordplay (BFHS), serving as its President from 1998–2004. He also in 1998 established Macdonald Armouries, where he continues to make handcrafted swords and knives.

Maestro Macdonald received his Master-at-Arms certification from the Italian Federation for Ancient and Historical Fencing (FISAS) in 1999 and established the Macdonald Academy of Arms in 2001. In early 2008, he founded the Commando D Living History Group, specialising in World War II combatives. Maestro Macdonald established the Conflicts of Interest battlefield archaeology group in 2015 and also continues to serve as a British Army Reservist.

BEN MILLER

Ben Miller is an American filmmaker and author. He is a graduate of New York University's Tisch School of the Arts, was the winner of the Alfred P. Sloan Foundation Grant for screenwriting, and has worked for notable personages such as Martin Scorsese and Roger Corman. For the last thirteen years, Miller has studied fencing at the Martinez Academy of Arms, one of the last places in the world still teaching an authentic living tradition of classical fencing. He has served as the Academy's *chef de salle*, and has authored articles for the Association of Historical Fencing, focusing on the fencing and dueling of the American colonial period. He is the author of *Irish Swordsmanship: Fencing and Dueling in Eighteenth Century Ireland* (New York: Hudson Society Press, 2017), and the editor of *Self-Defense for Gentlemen and Ladies: A Nineteenth-Century Treatise on Boxing, Kicking, Grappling, and Fencing with the Cane and Quarterstaff* (Berkeley: North Atlantic Books, 2015) containing the writings of the noted duelist and fencing master, Colonel Thomas Hoyer Monstery. He wrote the foreword to the republication of Donald McBane's classic martial arts treatise, *The Expert Sword-Man's Companion: Or the True Art of Self-Defence* (New York: Jared Kirby Rare Books, 2017). Miller's articles about fencing and martial arts history can be found on the websites *martialartsnewyork.org* and *outofthiscentury.wordpress.com*.

CPSIA information can be obtained
at www.ICGtesting.com
Printed in the USA
LVHW011915051118
595972LV00014B/268/P